W9-BAJ-689

Death by Suburb

Death by Suburb

*How to Keep the Suburbs
from Killing Your Soul*

David L. Goetz

HarperSanFrancisco
A Division of HarperCollinsPublishers

HarperCollins Web site: http://www.harpercollins.com
HarperCollins®, 📖®, and HarperSanFrancisco™ are
trademarks of HarperCollins Publishers

FIRST HARPERCOLLINS PAPERBACK EDITION
PUBLISHED IN 2007
Designed by Joseph Rutt

Library of Congress Cataloging-in-Publication Data has been ordered.
ISBN: 978–0–06–085968–8
ISBN-10: 0–06–085968–7

07 08 09 10 11 RRD(H) 10 9 8 7 6 5 4 3 2 1

Contents

Acknowledgments

This book is dedicated to my family, the perfect-enough immortality symbol: my wife, Jana, and Christian, Kira, Cory, and, of course, Cassidy, the golden retriever.

Special thanks to my wife for her furrowed brow whenever she listened to me read something I had just written. After I rewrote the section (just after storming off saying she just didn't *get* it), I always felt grateful for her verbal and nonverbal redlines.

Thanks also to Jennifer Merck, a suburban mom and professional social worker, who read the chapters during 2004, forcing me to think more critically. I needed every one of her comments.

A big thanks, finally, to Mickey Maudlin and the folks at Harper San Francisco for giving a shot to a writer with no platform.

The Thicker Life

My wife and I worship at Latte Temple most Sundays before heading to church, and recently a homeless man asked for a ride to the College Avenue train station as I climbed into my SUV with two coffees worth almost $9 in hand. I told him to jump in.

"Are you headed to church?" he said. "Everyone goes to church here. I do too."

I've often thought my 'burb, located a little over twenty miles west of downtown Chicago, could create a tasty tagline and positioning statement for its public relations brochures: WHERE EVEN THE HOMELESS HAVE A CHURCH HOME. There appear to be more churches in my community than pizza joints. That's quite a statement, because Wheaton, Illinois, is, after all, a suburb of Chicago, home to the world's best pizza. A church building fills at least one corner of most every intersection. On Sundays, high school auditoriums are rented by start-ups. Here is no shortage of houses of worship. I'm sure there must be some pagans in our community, but nobody has seen one in years, though I recently saw some Democrats at the Fourth of July parade. Wheaton is pretty much a God-and-country community.

I'm at church most every Sunday with my family. I play tepid electric guitar licks in the worship band for our "contemporary service." I don't give as much money as I should to the church, but I hope to after I make it big. And I fear that my lack of Bible reading may be the primary reason I feel such spiritual malaise while living the good life in my safe 'burb. Somebody just told me that 90 percent of Christians don't read their Bible every day. I sure don't. I've had a few good stretches, but I'm not in one now, and I've never read the Bible in one year, like my mom did. [I slid through a graduate theological education without reading every verse of the Bible. My religious tradition advises me to "get into the Word" (the Bible). And that, perhaps, is my problem: my knowledge is insufficient. But I have my doubts.]

My family and I live in a county that recently was ranked in the ninety-ninth percentile in the United States for quality of life. On most days, my biggest decision is lunch: the Atomic Turkey or the Veggie Panini? Our suburb, an older one of glorious hardwoods, harbors an intriguing mix of folks who can somehow afford its nosebleed housing prices (at least to a Midwesterner).

Plumbers live next to investment bankers. Fixed-income retirees, who bought their small ranch-style homes thirty or forty years before prices skyrocketed, live across the street from thirty-five-year-old bond traders who work in Chicago, who mortgaged their peace of mind to tear down a fifty-year-old, 1,200-square-foot ranch and erect a brick "starter castle." Everyone knows where "the apartments" sit along Route 38, near the local community college (one of the largest in the nation), and along north Main Street.

Our Mayberry public elementary school sits in white-skinned suburbia, though kids from section 8 housing just down the street and from a suburb to the north add to our children's experience of ethnic and economic diversity. An acquaintance told me that her neighbor yanked her first child out of the school after his kindergarten year, transferring him to a Christian grammar school. The woman apparently felt uncomfortable with all the kids from "the apartments" in little Johnny's class. "Too diverse," she said. "Besides, don't kids at the Christian school end up getting better SAT scores?"

Our elementary school has almost 20 percent less Caucasian kids than other District 200 schools. Enough to make a Security Mom nervous. I grew up in North Dakota, a state with virtually no diversity, except for a few Native Americans, who in times past we sequestered on a reservation. Today I inhabit a metropolitan area where a suburb nearby has a Hispanic population of almost 50 percent. Some suburbs are fast becoming almost as diverse as the cities.

There's no one-suburb-fits-all, of course. Not all suburbs are like mine. As far as I know, my suburb has not recently had first-graders getting busted with Baggies™ of crack in their backpacks, like another Chicago suburb. However, many 'burbs are arguably organized around the provision of safety and opportunities for children and neat, tranquil environs for homeowners. Suburbs and exurbs have grown to dominate the American landscape precisely because, most of the time, they fulfill those promises in spades. Throughout this book, whenever I refer to the suburbs or exurbs, I'm doing so in an archetypal sense.

In the introduction to *Crabgrass Frontier,* sociologist Kenneth T. Jackson writes, "The space around us—the physical organization of neighborhoods, roads, yards, houses, and apartments—sets up living patterns that condition our behavior."[1] What Jackson observed sociologically may also be true spiritually. Whether blue-collar or white, Yankee or Southern, west coast or east, North Dakota or southern Texas—the environment of the suburbs weathers one's soul peculiarly. That is, there are environmental variables, mostly invisible, that oxidize the human spirit, like what happens to the metal of an un-garaged car.

I think my suburb, as safe and religiously coated as it is, keeps me from Jesus. Or at least, my suburb (and the religion of the suburbs) obscures the real Jesus. The living patterns of the good life affect me more than I know. Yet the same environmental factors that numb me to the things of God also hold out great promise. I don't need to escape the suburbs. I need to find Jesus here.

Great first section!

'BURBIA WITH NO JESUS

Seven-year-old birthday parties in which the party favor your son scores on the way out costs twice as much as the gift he brought; the one-ton SUV in the driveway; the golden retriever with a red bandana romping with two children in the front yard; the Colorado winter vacations; the bumper sticker trumpeting "My daughter is an honor roll student at Hubble Middle School"—those are the dreams of the denizens, like me, of suburbia.

I've acquired most of those in the last fifteen years. I grew up in both North and South Dakota, where a regional cliché has it, "Even the jackrabbits carry lunch boxes." Ergo, even the wildlife think it's desolate. There's a lot of empty space. Even today, the suburbs seem noisy to me. My interior geography is windy and dry and desolate and spacious (empty, some might say).

I never really felt the need for an SUV or a golden retriever until I moved to a western Chicago suburb in my late twenties. The first few years, I silently mocked the young mothers of suburbia as they trucked their kids from home to school in oversized vehicles. I felt superior. I grew up with a minimalist mentality to security: in North Dakota, where the true rugged outdoors folk live, you don't need a four-wheel drive, even in −30° winters with a foot or two of snow. You need a pair of long underwear, a good shovel, and a modicum of luck. But as soon as I could, I financed my first SUV. I had to start a business, finally, to afford one, thanks to the tax write-off. And not just any SUV. It had to be one such that when I stopped at a red light, my cheeks would flush as I felt the gaze of the driver of the smaller vehicle beside me. Nothing is quite as satisfying as idling next to another large Child-Moving Vehicle when mine is bigger, no matter how much I have to pay for gas.

For reasons that largely escape me now, I chose out of the gate to pursue a career in Christian ministry. After college I took a year off and then spent the next four years (more or less) studying, working, and skiing, though not, necessarily, in that order. I enjoyed my seminary experience, but I felt ambivalent about whether I had been truly "called by God." I never felt like a preacher. And no one who listened to me preach begged me to do more of it. The headwaters of my ambivalence, I believe, originated in part from my religious tradition, which in various ways communicated to its young that the highest calling in life was to serve God in a "full-time" capacity as a pastor or missionary. That motivated me to endure the education for ministry, but after the degree, I jumped at a way out. Two years out of seminary, I got married, and eight months later Jana and I moved to the Chicago area to write and edit for a religious magazine publisher.

Over time, my suburban consciousness began to form. While assisting in my daughter's kindergarten class one afternoon, I read with the children. Each had a book that, when mastered, would be replaced with another. I read with my daughter, Kira, first, of course; she stumbled through the kindergarten-level book, but I felt good, even a little smug, about her progress. She is so advanced for her age. The next child, Trevor, breezed through a book that, as I learned a few minutes later, was at a fourth-grade level. I choked back my anxiety as I mumbled, "Great reading, Trevor." I don't think our eight-year-old could have read the book. At dinner, I announced to our family a Great Books Reading Program, effective immediately. No more television after dinner.

I absorbed quickly that my children's education needed to be approached like an NBA championship. No detail was too small and no standardized test too insignificant. Education was not really about learning but about winning. One day after report cards, a friend of my oldest (nine years old at the time) reprimanded me when I asked if he felt good about his report card: "My dad tells me that it's not nice to tell people your grades because some people don't get straight A's like I do."

I left publishing in 2000 to start a business just before the dot-com collapse, and then came the 9/11 sucker punch. I was not prepared for the spiritual darkness that ensued. Like all such small enterprises, for the first few years my small business hiccuped and gasped. I agonized like most naïve, undercapitalized entrepreneurs. It wasn't a struggle to survive so much as it was a struggle to experience Jesus in the midst of the disappointments. That surprised me. I was buoyed mostly by the goodness of spiritual friends. I was bewildered by my blindness to the reality of God. After years of religious activities, where was Jesus?

In one of Friedrich Nietzsche's more bizarre passages, in *Thus Spake Zarathustra,* Zarathustra himself speaks after some time in solitude. He sees (or visualizes) an ear: "An ear as big as a man!" Zarathustra looks closer and sees that the large ear is attached to a "small, thin stalk—

but this stalk was a human being!" Zarathustra goes on, "If one used a magnifying glass one could even recognize a tiny envious face; also, that a bloated little soul was dangling from the stalk."[2]

A bloated little soul—that's what I fear for my life, as I fill my early fall evenings with six-year-old soccer practices. Zarathustra calls that ghoulish image an "inverse cripple"—too much of one thing. The ear is out of whack, out of scale, with the rest of the human being. The suburbs tend to produce inverse spiritual cripples. Suburbia is a flat world, in which the edges are clearly defined and the mysterious ocean is rarely explored. Every decision gets planned out, like the practice of registering at retail stores for one's wedding gifts. Only tragedy truly surprises.

In the 'burb I inhabit, many are the opportunities for Bible study, innovative worship services, helping the homeless, children's programs, small groups, and much more. Yet I can't shake the image of the inverse cripple with a bloated, tiny soul. Perhaps that's one of the effects of comfortable suburban living. Too much of the good life ends up being toxic, deforming us spiritually. The drive to succeed, and to make one's children succeed, overpowers the best of intentions to live more reflectively, no matter the piety. Should it be any surprise that the true life in Christ never germinates?

It's in this environment that I've undertaken to discover the life Jesus describes in Matthew: "Are you tired? Worn out? Burned out on religion? Come to me. Get away with me and you'll recover your life. I'll show you how to take a real rest. Walk with me and work with me—watch how I do it. Learn the unforced rhythms of grace. I won't lay anything heavy or ill-fitting on you. Keep company with me and you'll learn to live freely and lightly" (Matt. 11:28–30, The Message).

That doesn't sound like my life, like my faith, like what even seems possible. Is the more reflective, more centered spiritual life truly available?

CURE FOR BLINDNESS

In my mid-twenties, while attending seminary, I cobbled together a living in the Denver, Colorado, metro area, part of what's known as the Front Range, where the eastern Colorado thinly grassed plain rumps and roils and then rises up into foothills and then into the Rocky Mountains. During the harsh light of midday, if a traveler stands on the plains and gazes westward toward the foothills and mountains, the landscape appears one-dimensional, flat, like the false storefronts of an old western movie. But in the softer, changing light of dusk, the foothills and mountains separate and emerge and fatten, take form. As darkness falls, the shadows lengthen and accentuate the canyons and flat irons and ridges. The landscape becomes multidimensional. The escaping light gives the traveler depth of field, a deeper, truer grasp of reality: in fact, the landscape is not at all flat; it's thick, layered, deep.[3]

This is the true nature of our life, even in the mirage that is my suburb. It is not a flat reality. In *Everest: The West Ridge,* mountaineer Thomas F. Hornbein writes about the thickness of reality—when at the top of a mountain he and his team awakened to another dimension of experience:

> We felt the lonely beauty of the evening, the immense roaring silence of the wind, the tenuousness of our tie to all below. There was a hint of fear, not for our lives, but of a vast unknown which pressed upon us. A fleeting disappointment—that after all those dreams and questions this was only a mountaintop—gave way to suspicion that maybe there was something more, something beyond the three-dimensional form of the moment.[4]

A life lived well spiritually, it seems, is a life lived in the thickness—in the space beyond and including the three-dimensional form of the moment. The harsh light of suburban living tricks us—our lives are anything but flat. One simply needs eyes to behold its thickness. The discipline, then, is learning to see again.

There are moments when our inner eyes flicker open. Sometimes a brush with death forces new vision. *Peak moments*—that's how *Outside* magazine described an "outsized moment, some breakthrough, I-just-didn't-realize instant when your relationship with the natural world pivots, expands, and is forever transformed."[5] A firefighter described how he was almost burned alive by a raging forest fire: "Chased by the fire, I ran like a madman, and then splashed into a low creek, where I drank, doused my head, and vomited. A revelatory moment, of sorts. I had been fighting fire all that summer, but I hadn't yet reckoned with its elemental power. Now I understood its deification—a terrible god of annihilation."[6] That reckoning changed him forever: "It was as though I had eaten from the Tree of Knowledge. My corporeality was clarified. I was no different from a rump roast, a ham. I was 19, and made of tender flesh."[7]

The outward physical world of SUVs and minivans, drearily earth-toned subdivisions, golden retrievers and chocolate labs, and endless Saturday morning soccer games is only one dimension. There's another dimension or two. This much thicker world is a world in which I am alive to God and alive to others, a world in which what I don't yet own defines me. It's a higher existence, a plane where I am not the sum total of my house size, SUV, vacations, kids' report cards—and that which I still need to acquire.

In *Mysticism,* early twentieth-century British writer Evelyn Underhill describes the moment when the "self, abruptly made aware of Reality, comes forth from the cave of illusion like a child from the womb and begins to live upon the supersensual plane."[8] The first step, then, is out of the cave, and it may begin, simply, with the awakening that comes from profound suffering or the simple admission that the suburbs are an illusion. It comes from a deep sense that something is wrong.

A NEW PLANE OF CONSCIOUSNESS

In *Mysticism,* Underhill writes that within each person there is an "immense capacity for perception, for the receiving of messages from the outside; and a very little consciousness which deals with them." The outside world drowns out what she calls "transcendental matters," or simply an awareness of one's spiritual consciousness. We use, in short, very little of the bandwidth for our God-consciousness. It has been in my most desperate moments, when shocked at the darkness in my soul, that I've felt most open to the presence of God. Yet I've also felt little confidence that I might experience God. Jesus simply didn't seem there. I didn't have the capacity for experiencing the presence of Christ.

For those of suburban Christian faith, developing the capacity for spiritual consciousness tends to be the forgotten frontier. At least that's true in the Protestant tradition in which I grew up and which I, for the most part, still inhabit. The kingdom of God belongs to the busy, to those who know how to work, to the spiritual entrepreneurs. The highest compliment to pay a young woman from the rural culture in which I was raised is: "She's a hard worker (and a good cook)." My suburban neighbors are a bit more sophisticated: "Mary is on the traveling soccer team and has the lead in the school play, and she has three hours of homework every night! Oh my God, can you believe it?"

Add to that the suburban environment of security, efficiency, and opportunities—and the overindulged self, which desperately needs all three—and spirituality morphs into activities: Bible studies, small group meetings, reading yet another best-selling book on the key to victorious Christian living, even serving at the local homeless shelter. It's the reverse, though, of what should happen. Such activities or practices should open our eyes to the larger world. Instead, they can obscure it. I've always felt cheered by the comment a friend made about his prayer life: he said he really didn't like the actual act of praying much, though he loved the open space that praying created in his life for God to work.

In *Pilgrim at Tinker Creek,* Pulitzer prize–winning writer Annie Dillard writes that "the mind's muddy river, this ceaseless flow of trivia and trash, cannot be dammed, and that trying to dam it is a waste of effort that might lead to madness."[9] The muddy river of suburban life cannot be stopped. It simply is. The muddy river of illusion cannot be escaped, really. There's not much use in moralizing about it, mocking it, thumbing your nose at it, treating it with light disdain—or sacrificing your way out of it (I'll drop everything and become a missionary or move to a Wisconsin cabin to live the simple life). I suppose some can take that path. I can't. My wife and I have a suffocating mortgage, three kids, and a decade of school plays and parent-teacher conferences before us. That itself feels like a heroic sacrifice. A friend recently groused to me about a speaker he had heard at a men's breakfast at his church. Apparently the speaker had challenged the men to "get out of their comfort zones." My friend snapped, "What comfort zone? I work all day in the corporate world, try to be a father and husband, and tithe and give some time to the church. If there's a comfort zone in that, I want to know about it!"

You can try to slow down your life, adjust your lifestyle downward, give more, pray more. Another study group, another stint on a church committee, another year as the nursery coordinator, another mission trip to a Third World country—all good things—but not necessarily superhighways to the deeper life. Dillard says that "instead, you must allow the muddy river to flow unheeded in the dim channels of consciousness; you raise your sights." She echoes much of the Christian mystic tradition through the centuries: You need to see better or, rather, awaken to a grander vision for your life.

The twist, though, is that you can't raise your sights by deciding to raise your sights. You can't really chase after the thicker life directly. For centuries, the classic spiritual disciplines and practices enlarged the capacity of ordinary people to engage the Sacred. Spiritual practices are not really a direct route to an awakened God-consciousness. Some days, they seem stupid, quite worthless, even just one of the many activities that keep me from God. Yet over time they awaken us to a brave new world that is, ultimately, more satisfying and true to who we are than is what we encounter without them.

The rap on Dillard's "raise your sights" idea, though, is that it's not enough. Doesn't Jesus require something more radical? Doesn't Jesus demand immediate results, fresh sacrifice, more *doing*?

"I just can't help but think that what you're suggesting is not enough," said a young mother who attended a church discussion group on spiritual practices for living in the suburbs. "There must be more. This [life of spiritual practices] lets people off the hook. It needs to be a more radical call to discipleship. It just feeds complacency."

But more what? More sacrifice? More church activities?

That doesn't sound much like the free and light life offered by Christ. It sounds more like the main character of Mel Gibson's *Braveheart.* The Protestant tradition loves the heroic call to sacrifice all for the kingdom of God. But the call to sacrifice often feeds, ultimately, mostly the ego. The New Testament doesn't characterize "thy kingdom come, thy will be done" as heroic. The kingdom is a mustard seed. The kingdom is a woman looking for a lost coin. The kingdom is a shepherd looking for lost sheep. The kingdom is a fourteen-year-old girl who breaks into a smile when she learns that her father just broke up with his lover, and now the teenager will have her father to herself for Christmas. The kingdom of God often appears plain, ordinary, small, in the moment.

Wow!

Not long ago I reconnected with a college buddy, now an executive for a software company. Through the years, I had heard sketchy details about his life from a mutual friend and knew that he and his wife were living in the West and had five kids. While on vacation one summer, my wife and I ended up at dinner with Tim and his wife, Cara. It was reassuring to find that Tim was still as outrageous as he was in college. Suburbia hadn't suffocated his larger-than-life personality. We learned that the couple, in their early forties, now had not five kids but six. They had acquired another since the last update.

This new one, though, was the same age as their oldest son. After a baseball tournament one summer, their oldest (then twelve) came to his father and said, "Dad, you remember Seth, don't you? Seth's got some trouble at home. Can he spend the rest of the day with us?" A few years earlier, Seth had played at their house before his family moved away.

That night, Tim and Cara couldn't get hold of Seth's mom. Seth stayed over. Then he spent another night. After several days, Cara finally tracked down Seth's mom, a single mom struggling with a drug habit and poverty. Apparently, Seth was virtually homeless, a twelve-year-old raising himself. Cara offered to have Seth stay a few more days if that would help her out. Seth's mom said that would be fine. Then she vanished for six weeks. Seth put his clothes in one of the dresser drawers. He arrived one Saturday after a baseball tournament and never left.

After the initial adrenaline rush of taking Seth in, Tim felt resentful: *I've got a twelve-year-old already, plus four others. How am I going to focus on two twelve-year-olds? I've got to be a dad to a kid I don't even know?*

"I had competitive thoughts," Tim said, "wanting my son to be better at baseball or whatever. Eventually I began to see Seth's need for me to love him as a son. I told myself, *This is something I've got to do; get over it.*" Tim was surprised that his son didn't seem to feel competitive for his attention. His oldest had, by inviting Seth in, voluntarily sacrificed his position in the family; he literally shared everything with Seth, including a room. Tim says that his son's compassion helped drain some of the resentment. "We never would have done this," said Tim, "if we had thought and prayed about it. It has become a hilarious social arrangement. People told us not to get involved because of the legal issues. We just didn't think about it much until we were too deep into it."

Four years later, Seth is like a son to Tim and Cara. They now have parental power of attorney, and Seth's mom lives nearby and joins in Seth's parenting now and again. Tim and Cara shrug off their choice as a little bit impulsive, in the moment, and something that they just had to do. In *The Sabbath,* Jewish writer Abraham Heschel says, "The higher goal of spiritual living is not to amass a wealth of information, but to face sacred moments.... [I]t is not a thing that lends significance to a moment; it is a moment that lends significance to things." Tim and Cara faced a sacred moment that probably did not appear as such. It was plain, ordinary—and right in front of them.

Tim and Cara *see* better than I do. I probably would have told my wife that we needed to pray about Seth's situation. Prayer is often a wonderful tactic to delay obedience. God would have had to figure something else out for Seth.

Even in suburbia all moments are infused with the Sacred. God really is present where I live on Ranch Road. Reality is not flat, but thick, deep, full. Here is another world which I need new eyes to see. This is a book about learning to see again. I don't need to escape the 'burbs to find Jesus. I need only awaken to the thicker life.

Each of the following eight chapters contains one spiritual practice or insight. The final chapter casts a vision for awakening to this new life. While I've chosen eight, there may, in reality, be twenty-eight. These eight practices and perspectives hold out the greatest possibility for transforming my bloated reality on Ranch Road. Within each chapter, I also narrate the stories of those who embody the practice or way of thinking. The stories give me hope—the thicker life is not just a fantasy. You don't have to hole up in a monastery to experience the fullness of God. Your cul-de-sac and subdivision are as good a place as any.

Inside Space

Environmental Toxin: "I am in control of my life."
Spiritual Practice: The prayer of silence

One fall Friday afternoon, while I watched our kids in the front yard, a cherry red Mercedes Benz convertible zoomed past and then slowed to a stop where our block dead-ends.

It was one of those rare Midwestern days when the temperature and humidity converge to perfection. The bright yellow and burnt red leaves of our street's hardwoods trembled in the light breeze. Only yards from the intersection, I could see the countenance of the convertible's driver, a late-middle-aged man with a full head of wavy silver hair. He glanced right and left and then right again. He couldn't make a left. A black hearse, cemetery bound, had just passed. Cars with little orange-and-black flags on their hoods crawled behind it. The man angrily threw his car in reverse, whipped it around, and accelerated to the opposite side of our block from whence he came. The irony was plain:

Everyone says: go faster. Everyone says: upgrade. Everyone says: be more efficient.... Faster and faster can only mean, in the end, stasis. The logical outcome of efficiency is uselessness.... No matter how quickly you move, death drives the fastest car on the highway. In the end, death always does the overtaking.[1]

Speed and efficiency rank high in suburban values. Garbage cans with properly colored tags are set out on the curb weekly on designated days. Dogs must be licensed before February 1. Dog waste is a hazard to our children, says our community publication on new ordinances. There are always new ordinances. Near our home, a gentleman walks his aging, bloated Labrador most evenings, dog leash in one hand and pooper-scooper in the other. By day, the man is an executive with an MBA from a world-class university; by night, he scrapes up dog stools.

Ha!

A few days after my wife and I moved to Glen Ellyn, Illinois, where we lived for four years, I sauntered next door to introduce myself to the neighbors. The husband, a blue-haired retiree, wore a white T-shirt and plaid slacks that stopped just short of his ankles. After grunting his name, his first burst of conversation ended with "I just want to let you know that in Glen Ellyn, you can't leave your car parked on the street at night."

A friend's "covenant community" in the West requires him to paint his patio home one of three or four earth-tone colors, but only after he gets permission: "The appearance of the community is of vital importance to the environment and to property values. . . . It will be necessary to submit a Design Review Request, even if you are painting your home the same color."

A colleague's preteen son had a sleepover. When the father of one of the boys arrived to pick up his son the next day, he called the house on his cell phone: "Could you have _____ come out; I'm in your driveway." A phone call beat the five-second walk to the front porch.

At one of our Park District pools, placards of rules adorn every piece of equipment—fences, slides, chairs—including the warning, "Additional Rules may be added, if deemed necessary by the management." "I hate going to that pool," says my five-year-old, "'cause you can't do anything there."

In the fall, at the local suburban pumpkin farm, young mothers who no doubt formerly managed human resource departments wait in line for live pony and tilt-a-whirl rides and moon jumps. They wait not only for their kids but for the kids of other mothers in the carpool. Why not wait in line for your kids *and* your neighbor's? Your own kids then never have to wait long. What a perfect world!

A friend replayed a home video of a family party several years ago and commented to me later that she was surprised at how little she seemed to enjoy what was happening in the video. In her anxiety to manage everything to perfection, she says she missed the actual moment— the birthday, the laughter, the joy.

One late winter morning, I sat in a coffee shop and planned my day. I stood up to leave and noticed the ice on the window. I stepped outside and caught sight of for the first time the saw-toothed frozen crystals on all the winter maples and hanging wires. It had rained and then snowed the night before. How could I have driven over early that morning and not really *seen* the fresh winter?

Busyness and efficiency stalk the deeper, spiritual life. I know that. Every spirituality guru and papyrus since the Desert Fathers trumpets that you can't live the deeper life *and* the busy life. You get one but not the other. But knowledge really doesn't change much. At least not for me or in me. I cannot envision a nonbusy, nonefficient life. I own a small business. Clients don't pay us to miss deadlines.

If you visit an eatery in most rural towns, you'll overhear seemingly inane conversations on the weather. Most folks who depend on the weather for their livelihood, whether farmers or small business owners who depend on the farmers, know intuitively that life can't be controlled.

The weather is an uncontrollable, arbitrary god that rains on the just and the unjust.

I'm not sure there is a comparable god in my suburb, where every child has the potential to attend Harvard, and every five-year-old soccer player has a parent who believes there exists a spot on the Olympic team for little Julia. And where size 4 moms with cropped hair carpool kids in cavernous SUVs because of a half-inch snowfall. I take note of the weather only to know whether to grab my umbrella when I commute into the city.

In a world that I will into being, there's not much need for mystery, for the Sacred, for that which is outside my control. Everything happens for a reason, right? If I want a better marriage, I attend the church's small group on marriage. If I want more knowledge of church history, I take a class at the local Christian college. If I want to protect my kids from bad music, I play in the minivan the Christian radio station that brands itself "Safe for the whole family." If Halloween scares me, my kids and I can attend a Fall Festival, an alternative Halloween event at a large church in our area; the scale and professionalism of the games and pony rides and pizza dwarf any secular alternative. I feel good about that. I live in a neighborhood that's so safe that the only way Christians "stand up for Christ" is by not serving alcohol at the block party. (It's a family neighborhood, after all!) Even the construction workers working on the new $1 million home next door listen only to nice Christian radio. How nice for our kids!

Immersed in a context that values things done right or not at all, I inevitably conclude, mostly subconsciously, that I can control my life. True spirituality is the opposite of control, though, for in the end death always does the overtaking. You miss that fact and you miss the larger purpose of spiritual formation.

The deeper spiritual life is never a direct route. If it were, religion in the suburbs would be the fast track to the Godhead, given the First World's entrepreneurial and managerial bent. I could just control my way to Jesus. In the toxic dump of efficiency and control, though, the first act must be countercultural—a decision not to act. This is the first spiritual practice. A choice to listen and wait for God. Making time for space for God is the most basic element of spirituality. You can't stop your busyness, really. You begin to open your life to God in small amounts. You don't need a condo in Beaver Creek or a monk's cell on the grounds of a rural retreat. You don't need to go anywhere. You need just a modicum of will to begin the practice of solitude and swim upstream against the suburban current.

SPIRITUAL MAGNETITE

Each spring, monarch butterflies migrate northward from Mexico to the United States. In their eight-hundred-mile journey, they can encounter winds of up to fifty miles an hour. Some die of exhaustion, others of starvation, but amazingly, most stay on course to complete the trip. In addition to using an internal compass to "monitor the sun's position and maintain a northerly direction," monarch butterflies "home in on the chemical odor of billions of fallen butterfly scales at lepidoptera-friendly rest stops en route." And they "use traces of magnetite in their wings to detect magnetic charges in the rocks."[2]

For two thousand years, Christian spiritual practices have functioned like magnetite to guide the spiritually minded through the ten thousand joys and ten thousand sufferings of life.[3] The practice of solitude may be the most important spiritual discipline for the suburbs. And it is probably one of the most difficult to practice here. At least with a Bible study or a small group, I am forced into the discipline by the fact that I have to attend something. But with solitude, there's no penalty for missing the practice. Life goes on. No real damage. One day you arise and discover you wouldn't know if God was at work even if there were handwriting on your wall. You have no capacity for seeing God.

When I think of solitude, I fantasize about moving my family from our Midwestern suburb to a small town in the western United States edged by a rambling stream and cradled in the foothills of a mountain range with a romantic name like the Spanish Peaks. There we'd live out our days in simplicity and natural beauty and with few financial anxieties. Life would be fully aligned. Our frenetic life would slow to a manageable pace. God would be easier to detect.

But I know that what glistens in my mind is a phantasm; I know what small towns are like. I grew up in mostly rural communities whose most notable architectural landmarks were the county courthouse and the Tastee-Freeze and whose denizens suffered from poverty and isolation. My high school senior class numbered seventeen. At least in the North and South Dakota prairie soil in which I sprouted, God did not seem nearer because of the environment. And if beauty and solitude are preliminary to the deeper life, then why does the mountain state region in the United States have such high rates of suicide? What good, then, is creation?

While growing up in the Dakotas, my environment and outdoor hobbies seemed to obviate the need for solitude. A colleague once called the Chicago suburbs "the land of no horizons." Power lines, the dormers on a neighbor's Cape Cod, and mature hardwoods obstruct the full evening's redness in the west. The day's final beauty is always about an hour away. I commute to the country (that is, the cornfields) to view the stars. My children learn about animals in the fall by riding ponies that circle a pole at the local suburban pumpkin "farm." One of my first pets was a real black and white Shetland pony named Topsy, which would stand idly when I fell off.

Solitude tends to be romanticized in the 'burbs and is bundled up with creation: "I wish I had five acres where I could run a horse or two, have a St. Bernard, and live more simply." One of the inspirations for the planned suburb, in fact, in America was "the large suburban cemeteries that began to be built just outside city centers in the 1930s."[4] When friends recently moved from a suburb near ours to a development almost forty-five minutes farther west where corn rows abut their neighbor's property, I hid my envy poorly. I suddenly felt anxious when a friend who lives on the outskirts of Denver, in foothills of pine trees and wandering deer and elk, told me he had just purchased a piece of property for a cabin deep in the Colorado backcountry. How could I make that happen for our family?

Across the busy street from the townhouse complex where my wife and I purchased our first suburban property is the Prairie Path, a recreational artery that cuts through the western suburbs. Near where we lived, it threads its way between a trailer park that seems out of place in our pristine suburb and a swamplike area of cat-tails and winter-killed grass, and then crosses a muddy stream to disappear around a stand of hardwoods. The Prairie Path became a sanctuary in my suburban wilder-ness. It was the place I wandered to find solitude, to pray, and to listen for the still small voice of God.

I learned quickly, however, that the Prairie Path was no sanctuary. Rush hours are from mid-morning Satur-day through Sunday evening, spring through fall; hun-dreds riding titanium mountain bikes and sporting purple and black spandex and white helmets grunt, "Left," as they pass the runners and walkers. Weekend Prairie Path traffic is worse than Chicago's Eisenhower Expressway on a late Friday afternoon. When a white-tailed deer bounds across the path, gapers become a prob-lem. I've often thought radio stations could provide a great service with crowd reports.

With no outside space, I've often felt like our friends' preteen son who can't concentrate. He says he feels like "New York City's in my brain."

RELINQUISHING CONTROL

While I esteem the saints throughout history who aban-doned the cities to draw close to God in the quiet and in nature, most who live in the suburbs and cities can't follow them. A few can, but family and career choices early on for most obviate a more contemplative life. If the getaway-from-it-all model of spirituality is the high road, then most ordinary suburban folk, wedged in cloned subdivisions, can expect to find God only on weekends in Wisconsin.

While outdoor solitude is a premium, it is not necessary for learning to uncover eternity in the ordinary. Nature and beauty are add-ons to Christian spirituality—nice but not necessary. Nature, in one sense, is overrated. It can provide a context for a spiritual explorer to listen for God, but it cannot teach the deeper truths. In *The Four Loves,* C.S. Lewis writes, "If you take nature as a teacher, she will teach you exactly the lessons you had already decided to learn; this is only another way of saying that nature does not teach."[5] Several centuries earlier, reformer Martin Luther said essentially the same thing: "Nature cannot reveal God. Nature is indeed very wonderful, and every particle of creation reveals the handiwork of God, if one has the eyes to see." But nature can only confirm one's prior belief "in the beneficence of God."[6]

For spiritual development and entrance into the thicker, more reflective life, solitude is more inside space than it is outside space. Solitude isn't something to consume, like a summer vacation at Lake Tahoe. The answer to finding solitude isn't to physically flee the suburbs, to move farther west to another plain-vanilla subdivision next to a cornfield. It begins incrementally with the practice of becoming still. For a minute, for two minutes, for five minutes—not necessarily in beholding a snowcapped mountain peak, but simply in stopping the pursuit of efficiency. To stop being, if only for a few moments, the Lord of the Suburb. And to stop the scheming inside my head.

I often find solitude of any amount unrewarding. When I muster the discipline to spend time in silence, my expectations are rarely met. I want God to dole out clear directions about his will for my life. The Book of James seems to imply that the technique is quid pro quo: "Come near to God and he will come near to you" (Jas. 4:8): I find time for God, and God speaks to me during this time. Yet I've found the quid pro quo method doesn't seem to work, at least on the face of it.

That's the rub: if I can will my world into existence, then I should be able to will God into conversation. I read scripture, desperate for something to strike fire. Thoughts twinkle in my head. Catholic theologian Henri Nouwen admits, "It's not easy to sit and trust that in solitude God will speak to you—not as a magical voice but that he will let you know something gradually over the years."7

It's that "over the years" part that bothers me. I really don't have time for that. Mostly solitude is one tactic in the war to relinquish control. I can't control that my son didn't get asked to the birthday party of the summer, and I can't control the outcome of my daughter's MRI for a possible brain tumor. Or that of my son's two weeks later. A year later, when he needs yet another MRI, I still have no say-so in the matter. Ultimately, there's not much in my control. I am not Lord of the Suburb.

The life practice of solitude, then, is the opposite of my expectations of escape and rest or an immediate ushering into what I think is God's presence. It is more a discipline of struggle than it is of serenity. It's no formula for controlling my outer world or how I feel. It's the ongoing guerrilla war to loosen my choke hold on creating and gathering to myself the life I think I need. I don't pursue giving up control; I pursue the practice of solitude.

UNEXPECTED PROVISION

One spring in the mid-1990s, I traveled to Russia to spend a little more than a week with leaders in St. Petersburg and Moscow. A college professor and I were asked to teach at a small conference for Russian pastors. I had been to Russia twice before and jumped at the opportunity to go again. When my traveling companion, someone whom I hadn't met before, had a heart attack shortly before the trip, I debated whether to back out. To go meant I'd be alone for most of the trip. But my trip had been paid by a small organization, and I felt no small sense of obligation. I also reasoned the trip would provide me with some much-needed space to be alone.

I packed a novel, a book on socioeconomic conditions in Russia since 1989, a Bible, and a journal, and went alone. I planned to fly into St. Petersburg, spend a few days at a college there, then catch the all-night train from St. Petersburg to Moscow, something I was warned against because of the high crime rate. I would meet up with some Americans (whom I also didn't know) in Moscow for the last half of the trip.

When I arrived at the St. Petersburg airport, no one held up a sign with my name on it. Several appeared to look Western, and I asked, "Are you here to meet Dave Goetz?" Stony stares. I waited for my luggage, and when I cleared customs, I milled around until I overheard someone speaking English—and saw an American couple who were at the airport to meet someone else. I pushed my way over to them and discovered a Russian standing near them with a sign with my name. The front of the sign had been face down. I was grateful to find my ride (a

Russian cabbie), and from that point onward, I began to count the hours until I returned home.

During my time in St. Petersburg and Moscow, I met some wonderful Russians, a friendly South African who was teaching English in St. Petersburg, and a beautiful Ukrainian family of six. But the nine days away from my family were some of the loneliest of my life. One reason may have been several decisions awaiting me back home. I couldn't shut off my anxiety. I returned to Chicago the day my first son took his first steps. A week later, however, I continued to feel flat and suffered from a deep sense of feeling alone.

About two weeks after my trip, around 4:30 A.M., I was waiting for a colleague to take me to the airport. We planned to catch an early flight out of O'Hare. I had a few moments to spare before Kevin arrived, so I sat on the couch in our family room in silence that was almost as deep as the silence I once experienced when a snowmobile I was riding broke down in a secluded North Dakota pasture, miles away from the nearest farm, on a bitter cold, starry night in January. I felt as if I were in deep space. I don't remember how long I sat on the couch that morning—perhaps only ten minutes—but up through the silence into my consciousness a sentence formed: "I will provide." My head began to throb with the phrase. The fact that the sentence was in the first person—and not the third, "*God* will provide"—threw me at first, until it hit me who *I* was.

After the initial shock and euphoria of "hearing" God speak to my spirit, I began to look for ways God was providing. Especially in the first few years of starting my business, I expected God to sweep in dramatically and make me successful. That is what happens when God's at work, right? I look around: God seems to be providing big-time for others.

I have a harsh streak embedded in my personality, as my wife and kids will attest. When things seem to be floating along well, I can give off a laid-back aura—a fun-loving suburban dad who assists with Park District baseball and serves as a charismatic timer at swim meets. But under the surface is, nearly always, a roiling sea of emotion. I work my life to the edges. I can't imagine my life without stress. If there's no fire burning, I start one.

When business cash flow gets tight, my boiling point lowers, as my wife describes it. An argument with her under those conditions, for example, goes from a 3 to a 7: "Someone has to worry about money!" I like to think I'm normal, a generally decent person, and that to run a small business requires this kind of anxiety. I struggle to sync what I believe God revealed to me clearly—"I will provide"—with my often unchallenged belief that, in reality, I provide for myself. I don't really trust God's provision. If I did, would I lash out at those closest to me when receivables go long? Would I go off on my son's baseball coach and tell him to stop bitching at my son if I truly believed that God was sufficient for my life?

So I thought initially that "I will provide" was practical—a promise, really. I thought if God would solve the situational piece, I could live more peacefully. It has not worked that way. "I will provide" has never really afforded, to date, much in the way of practical help. And that's why "I will provide" has been so perplexing. It's a theme that keeps resurfacing as I cycle up and down with my business, with my marriage, with my children. As I grow tired of controlling my life, I wonder what it might mean to live with inner peace, the kind that comes only from God.

Solitude has at times disturbed me, raising more questions than supplying answers. When I find time for solitude in my suburb, I can think about the deeper motivations of my crazy life: Why does money mean control and power to me? Why am I so competitive with so-and-so? Inside space is the prayer of stillness. It may be the only kind of prayer that can unseat my reign as Lord of my Suburb.

In *The Sabbath: Its Meaning for Modern Man*, Abraham Heschel writes, "The answer to the problem of civilization: not to flee from the realm of space; to work with the things of space but to be in love with eternity."[8] Falling in love with eternity is staying and creating space in one's life for solitude. It may be as simple as getting up earlier each morning or buying a decent pair of ear plugs, but creating space is as necessary as setting up a line item for Christmas gifts in one's personal budget throughout the year. Without it, the January credit card bill will inevitably spike. Without a line item for quietness, the days get used up carpooling, working on another degree, making partner in the firm, planning yet another birthday party. One awakes some morning and finds that three years have slipped by. It's like noticing one early fall day that your three-year-old can finally pump his legs and swing by himself. He no longer needs you. It happened when you were not paying attention. Perhaps many dreams have been fulfilled—a move to a larger house, to vice president, to a condo after the kids have finally moved out—but the soul has become like a boarded-up discount store in an empty parking lot with weeds rising up out of the pavement cracks.

A middle-aged friend and mother of three spent three months in central Africa. When she returned, she said she missed the quiet evenings with no electricity and nothing to do. "I want to feel that silence again," she says. "All my normal ways of relaxing fell away: a glass of wine, listening to the radio or watching TV, calling a friend, going shopping, eating out." She now says she's much less driven to be with people. She's more okay with being alone.

Inside space is a mustard seed, "the smallest of all seeds, but it becomes the largest of garden plants and grows into a tree where birds can come and find shelter in its branches" (Matt. 13:32, New Living Translation). Inside space is a hidden treasure. It is the choice pearl. Over a lifetime, it liberates me from the illusion that I am in control of my life. Inside space, finally, invites me into the goodness and mysteries of God.

Scuffle with the Self

Environmental Toxin: "I am what I do and what I own."
Spiritual Practice: The journey through the self

The assignment was simple enough: Stay up late one night and observe the stars and write down what you see. Add the page to your science journal. Do it by November 1. The science teacher then cautioned her seventh-grade class, "Don't wait until the last night to do this. It's often cloudy that last week of October."

Sure enough, Halloween week was overcast. A few students handed in an incomplete journal. One completed assignment, however, raised an eyebrow of the teacher. At the top of the paper, it read: "At 2:03 A.M. on November 1, the clouds parted, and my son and I observed the stars for 25 minutes."

The teacher, a friend, said the constellations were poorly described and in the wrong part of the sky. The parent had done, of course, what any self-respecting 'burban parent would do: ensure the success of his child. Too bad one part of the overall score was for honesty. It was not the teacher's rookie year.

In one of his short stories, William Kittredge invents an illness called antidysthanasia. A female character dies from the disease, which Kittredge defines as the failure to take positive efforts to preserve life. In his autobiographical *Hole in the Sky,* Kittredge, who is no friend of faith, writes about his own self-destructive tendencies: "I knew nothing more valuable than self, which is another definition of antidysthanasia."[1] Antidysthanasia is behind much of the drive to make suburban children succeed. Why, for example, is Park District baseball so important that perfectly sensible, normal fathers snarl at their sons' nine-year-old teammates when the team starts to lose?

The *self* is a dominant theme in religion, and for good reason. The unawakened *self* lives only in the flat, mysteryless, empirical world, in pursuit only of what psychologist Ernest Becker called "immortality symbols." In *Escape from Evil,* he writes,

> Money gives power now—and, through accumulated property, land and interest, power in the future.... The symbols of immortal power that money buys exist on the level of the visible, and so crowd out their invisible competitor.... No wonder economic equality is beyond the imagination of modern, democratic man: the house, the

car, the bank balance are his immortality symbols.[2]

An immortality symbol is not really about the thing.
It's not about baseball. It's not really about my child. It's
about the glory that the thing bestows on me. I will be
famous, finally. I will have the masses bow down and
then rise up and call me Lord. Why do I feel so blessed
that my son has the best batting average on his Park
District team for a handful of spring games? Is it simply
because I'm proud of my son's accomplishments? Of
course not.

Successful children are the ultimate glory in today's
Park District and Travel Team culture. Children level the
playing field. Whether from blue money or new money
or no money, each child represents real potential for glory
in the here and now. They are the ultimate extension of
our selves. If glory means covering for your seventh-
grader, then so be it. Parenting is hard these days; perhaps
it truly is, as the saying goes, today's most competitive
adult sport.

The meaning of children and their accomplishments
is only one suburban immortality symbol. There is the
sprawling five-thousand-square-foot house with the gor-
geous sun porch. There is the "Ken and Barbie" appearance that some couples exude—eternal youth packaged

in fresh cleavage and low body fat. [For clergy, it's the three-thousand-member mega-church.] I wrote and edited for a clergy publication for several years. I often sat in the studies of both small-church pastors and mega-church pastors, listening to their stories, their hopes, their plans for significance. I deduced, albeit unscientifically, that often clergymen in midlife had worse crises of limits than did other professionals. Religious professionals went into the ministry for the significance, to make an impact, called by God to make a difference with their lives. But when you're fifty-three and serving a congregation of 250, you know, finally, you'll never achieve the large-church immortality symbol, the glory that was promised to you. That can be a dark moment—or a dark couple of years.

There is, frankly, no one more uninteresting than a person with no immortality symbols: the suburban family with no smart or athletic kids that lives in a relatively small house; the poor; the single mom left to raise three kids under twelve after the divorce; the elderly with no winter condo in Florida; the head of household with no real career track; the midlife pastor with a small congregation. None of these folks is asked to speak at the college alumni banquet.

I want to minister to these people

The quest for immortality is mostly about the care and feeding of the self. It's the unreflective pursuit of such symbols that creates the inverse cripple, the bloated tiny soul. Go ahead and study the Bible until you can quote most every passage, but if you avoid the journey through the self, you'll still end up on—as Franciscan Richard Rohr calls it—the embittered journey near the end of life. Knowledge has its own Law of Diminishing Returns.

There's no way to the presence of Jesus without the dying to self. This is an inward (not outer or pietistic) process. Christian spirituality writers describe it as an ongoing scuffle with the self. Religions frame the subject quite differently. The Christian faith, for example, speaks largely of "surrendering the self." Eastern Orthodox bishop Anthony Bloom best expressed the Christian view of this "purification process," saying that it is not "a journey into my own inwardness, it is a journey *through* my self, in order to emerge from the deepest level into the place where He is, the point at which God and I meet" (emphasis mine).[3]

To go deep into the presence of Christ, I must go within. I must learn to surrender my self. I find God through my self, in that place where there is union with the True Reality of the Universe. This suburban practice is a journey of prayer unlike any other prayer. It's listening not for the voice of God but for the voice of self. And then allowing the self to die of benign neglect.

JOURNEY WITHIN

prayer

My mother, a Seventh Day Adventist, and my father, a reborn Congregationalist, together raised five kids in a pietistic, nondenominational Protestant home. [Prayer was a blue-collar activity. Prayer worked. People of faith prayed and talked about prayer, and about the importance of praying more. You exhibited the worst kind of unbelief if you doubted for a moment that more prayer could heal someone or transform a hopeless situation.]

I rarely heard much, then, about a different kind of praying, about the journey through the self. It wasn't something rural-minded, nondenominational folk thought about much. Or perhaps if we did pray that way, we didn't have the language for it.

Nor did I pick up much on prayer in my twenties while attending seminary, where prayer is mostly for taking finals. Somewhere in my thirties I picked up the popular notion that prayer is essentially a casual, ordinary conversation with Jesus. I can start my day with God in the shower while rinsing off: "Good morning, Lord, thanks that Jana got up with the baby all three times last night." Or I could talk to Jesus while picking up some coffee: "Please help me find a parking spot right in front of Starbucks; it's really chilly today." I felt a little guilty about that prayer, though. I tried to reconcile mine with the prayer of a teenage mother in a Middle Eastern refugee camp who only needs a little food for her three children. I love the idea and practice of talking to Jesus about anything anywhere. I always wonder, though, if Jesus thinks I'm a descendant of Narcissus.

Not until I began reading some saints outside my religious tradition did I discover another world of prayer. Many of the Western classics on Christian spirituality were written by ascetics, by those who in one way or another took up more extreme forms of poverty, chastity, and obedience. They said no in a big way to the visible, external world. Many abandoned the good life to devote themselves to seeing the truer world. I've always been impressed that most Christian mystics end up back in the world serving the poor. There must be something about beholding the Holy within that pushes you back to the street. Rare are the Security Contemplatives or Gated Monks, with no skin in the game. Rather, they "gate" themselves only to go back into the street, to confront suffering, to serve the poor and the broken. It's "gating with a purpose."

I was surprised at how much the cloistered and hermitic saints still had to write about. The ascetic life no doubt garroted a few sins of flesh, but apparently the deeper life didn't end up easier, really, in an abbey. You have to work on it wherever you end up. In a cloister, alone in a cave, or on the sidelines of a soccer field, screaming at your eight-year-old to hustle. Bully for you if you can hone your devotional life at your summer cottage on Lake Michigan. But you may as well be hauling your kids to swim lessons. John the Baptist crystallized this process in what would make a decent message for a public relations campaign: "He [Christ] must increase, I must decrease" (John 3:30, King James Version).

UNDERGROUND RESISTANCE

Inside space is much easier to sell to suburbanites like me than is the ongoing scuffle with self. Who doesn't want to find more time to listen for God's voice, for deep and silent prayer? A spiritual retreat sounds good right about now, as long as the rooms have cable. *so true...*

Much less inspirational is the hand-to-hand combat with antidysthanasia, a necessary but tricky part of staying awake to the real world. Near the end of his life, novelist Frederick Buechner's hermit character in *Godric* attests to the difficulty of his life of solitude. Reflecting on his life in the third person, he says, "Godric's war is all within. For fifty years, the only foe he's battled with has been himself. Above all else he's prayed."[4]

The war within—the battle with the self—is really prayer itself. It's the long struggle to see Goodness and Beauty in a bogus world.

The wife of an acquaintance was recently diagnosed with cancer, and during her first week of chemo the husband dutifully shouldered the additional load at home. He trucked the kids to all their sporting and other after-school events. The stress of her uncertain future, of managing the entire family schedule for the first time, and of trying to run his small business unraveled him emotionally. Weeks before he had promised to substitute for the soccer coach at a Saturday game. In his newly defined reality, the elementary-age girls' soccer game took on increasing insignificance.

He noticed midway through the game that one of the players had vanished from the sidelines. Later he learned why: the parents, upset that he had played their daughter too little, had packed up their soccer chairs and stormed home. He thought he had rotated all the players through. He said he didn't say much to the wife when he called later for damage control.

Soccer is stupid when you think your wife is dying. The pettiness of suburban living shocks you, enrages you. The problem, of course, is that you can't live with that kind of intensity for long. The pettiness is so clear for a time, but then not so clear. Your clarity on what is real fades. For many in the 'burbs, life is less about the extremes (the really bad or the really good) and more about the middle. Most of the spadework of spirituality is done between the extremes. It's tough to see the thicker world on an average day with an average temperature when your kids just got their report cards and no one is really Harvard bound but yet they're all at least getting Bs. You should feel thankful. You don't. No one wants a child who makes only Bs, but hey, she's trying her best, right? That's all you ask of your kids. At least none, uh, has special needs.

To win the war within is to see that not only is soccer stupid when you think your wife is dying of cancer, it's really stupid, period. Not the game itself, of course. The game is good, even holy. It's stupid only when it becomes my immortality symbol. When the game becomes about me, what seventeenth-century French Catholic bishop François Fénelon called "self-love."

Fénelon was a bishop with a thing for Jesus. He was in and out of favor with his beloved Catholic church, which didn't fully appreciate Fénelon's emphasis on the deeper life. Fénelon was a friend of Jeanne Guyon, another French Catholic mystic, who was imprisoned for her views on the deeper Christian life. Fénelon's primary contribution to the contemplative life was arguably his insight into the self, which he describes as the inner voice "that suggests you live for yourself. The voice of self-love is even more powerful than the voice of the serpent."[5] Fénelon, of course, is pre-Freud, pre–modern psychology. He'd have few quarrels, I think, with today's notions of self-worth. Fénelon was out for bigger fish.

He believed, as most contemplatives did, that the old self lives on after a spiritual awakening. The awakening to the real, more true world triggers a fierce conversation between the old self and the new, what Godric called the war within. The old refuses to recognize the new. The journey within, then, is listening not only for the voice of God but for the voice of self-love. The spiritual practice is just as much prayer as is silence, as waiting for God to speak. Recognizing the voice of self-love is part of the odyssey deep within.

Why is it so important for my daughter to win the Reflections contest at school? Why does it make me feel so good that my sons are tall for their age (other than the fact that I've always been just shy of medium height)? Why am I blind to those I perceive to have less than I have? Why do I keep such a sharp eye on those with just a little more than I?

Why am I so bothered that the gift my six-year-old brought *to* her friend's birthday party was worth perhaps a tenth of the goodies that she brought *home* from the party: a chalk caricature of her drawn by an artist hired by the party mom, a long-stemmed rose, a plastic tiara, a cardboard princess purse, a Mylar balloon, four candy necklaces, and an emerald ring? [You know you're a suburban loser when your personal immortality symbol is your daughter's gift at a six-year-old's party.] Hs!

I once worked with a client who had on his business card "Reputation Management"; he was a consultant to large universities with public relations problems, like a student who had died of alcohol poisoning or been molested by a football player. I thought about hiring him to manage my suburban life. Self-love masks itself in a million ways, and image management is another form of antidysthanasia. A friend with a special needs child (and five other kids as well) recently said to me that he thought one spiritual issue of our community (which has a median household income of $75,000)[6] is how hard we work at appearing not to have any issues. "The sad thing," he says, "is that you wind up with a bunch of folks who appear to have it all, but are miserable. They're trapped in the attractive veneer of being 'perfect people.' That, by its very nature, negates the transparency to form a deeper bond with a human being."

I know in theory that the perfect life doesn't exist, but I want certain people to think that I'm a dedicated father with smart, athletic kids; a loving husband who will now and then clean a toilet and vacuum a carpet (though not dust a shelf); a swashbuckling entrepreneur who has gone from ashes to riches; a spiritual leader in the church who prays a lot, and gives a lot.

In preening my exceptional life, self-love does suburbia in a big way. It's part of the evolutionary human instinct for happiness that must be killed. [Suffering, of course, is self-love's natural predator, and this is where Fénelon's insights are most poignant.]

Fénelon's oeuvre includes collections of short letters written to those he was guiding spiritually. While Fénelon could write to comfort, he often cut to the bone. He could be tart. He seemed to think that it isn't the ostensibly big sins that trip us up. ["To just read the Bible, attend church, and avoid 'big' sins—is this passionate, whole-hearted love for God?"[7] When I read that, I wondered if Fénelon had just bought the mansion next door in my church-sated, piety-conscious community. I can think of only two big sins in our community: having an affair with your neighbor's wife or having to step down from your church leadership position because of your pornography habit. Both, when public, are quite embarrassing, nicking your perfect-life veneer. From what I've observed, my tradition seems mostly okay with driving SUVs (many of the 'burban pastors I know sport them), taking Cancun vacations, and buying homes with suffocating mortgages (a sign of God's blessing?).]

The vectoring spiritual issue for the deeper life is not

the big sins. They are what they are. You design your own suffering, and the consequences reverberate. The core issue, though, is recognizing the many faces of the self. Twentieth-century British novelist and essayist C. S. Lewis argued that pride was the greatest sin: "When I was talking about sexual morality, I warned you that the centre of Christian morals did not lie there. . . . [T]he essential vice, the utmost evil, is Pride."[8] Pride is one face of the self, and those who ignore it in their spiritual development win the prize of a bloated, distended soul at the end of life.

The subject of pride and its cousin, image management, really doesn't come up much. I don't confess to my religious community, "You know, I really need your prayers. I really feel prideful that my son won so many swimming medals this summer." Instead, I annoy my friends: "I'm so glad Christian has at least one sport that he's really good at. Did I tell you this past summer that he won medals in both the butterfly and the freestyle? He thinks he's the next Michael Phelps. . . . Ha, ha, ha. Isn't that cute? He's becoming such a little athlete."

I'm not simply a doting father in love with his son. I'm trying to convey something much more important: I have acquired an immortality symbol. I know this to be true because of the anxiety I feel when one of my kids gets B's instead of A's. I begin to crack down at home.

Just the other evening, my wife turned to me and said, "Is there something wrong with this picture? We're working on Christian's political science project for school, and he's in his room playing his Game Boy." Jana and I were proud when we got an A on his project.

The only real antidote to the anxiety of self-love is the cross, says Fénelon. The process is spiritual crucifixion, described in different ways throughout the centuries by the spiritually wise. The cross basically signifies suffering, and it comes in many shapes and sizes. In a later chapter, I will discuss what it means to come to terms with your allotment of suffering in this life. For now, my anxiety simply shows that some piece of my self still needs to die. The hurting is part of the dying. "Much of God's work is done in secret," writes Fénelon, "because you would not die to yourself if He always visibly stretched out his hand to save you."[9] In short, I would not die to my self if my kids always got A's, if they always made the varsity or traveling soccer team, if my business always grew at least 30 percent each year, if my marriage was truly as good as I tried to make it appear to others.

One marking of the thicker life, then, is the imperfect life—and it's the perfect antidote to self-love. The perfect suburban life is bogus. It's what the old self thinks is real. It's a lie, a sham, an illusion. The old self thinks that my neighbor, who just got promoted to president of the firm, is closer to the kingdom of God than I. The truth is that my other neighbor, who lost his job and ended up out of work for a year, is likely closer to the kingdom of God than is the president. I envy the president, I pity the unemployed: "I'll pray for you." *wow*

That is precisely why I feel perfectly righteous in storming off in the middle of a soccer game when my daughter doesn't get to play. There's so much more at stake than soccer. I want to believe—or perhaps I need to believe—that the family who embodies the perfect suburban life experiences real life. I want to believe that the man who, each Sunday, can fly his family in his Learjet to attend the church of his choice in another major metropolitan city really lives a better life than I. What if he really does?

The struggle of the self to disentangle itself from illusion is the real journey within. And that is the spiritual practice: accepting the imperfect life, with fewer immortality symbols. The imperfect life is the only life worth living. It is, in fact, the only life that anyone really lives.

LET IT HURT

Just the other day, I humiliated my oldest minutes before driving to O'Hare for a business trip. He had gotten an average grade. He called it "medium." He said it with tears in his eyes. "Medium?" I said. "Medium isn't good enough in this family!"

It was a tender family moment, and I was sorry I couldn't stick around to experience its fullness. But as I raised my voice and virtually screamed the word *medium* to my son, I had an almost out-of-body experience. It was as if I were hovering above the dining room and watching in slow motion as the conversation unfolded. In my head, I desperately wanted to keep my mouth shut, to let it go, to give my son a hug before I left, but I couldn't. I was carried along by a deeper current. As soon as I mouthed the words, I regretted them. I gave myself a thousand lashings while I drove to the airport.

The hard truth, of course, is that *medium* isn't good enough because I feel medium. I loathe medium. I want to be Lord. No, I *must* be Lord.

This is the point where Fénelon's spiritual direction is so poignant. When you're in this moment, Fénelon says, when you're outraged at your self, disgusted at your behavior, you must let it hurt. The hurting is part of the dying. In fact, Fénelon would say that the frustration I have with myself for what I did shows how much self-love I have. I'm shocked at my behavior. Fénelon says that's the real problem—the outrage at what I said. The problem is not so much that I went off on my son but that I felt so bad afterward. I think I'm more righteous than that. Fénelon would say, "You're not. You're self-righteous, and that's your big problem. So let it hurt. There's a future for you."

You know you've made some progress with your problem immortality symbol when you stop being shocked at your stupidity. Perhaps the next milestone is growing less anxious about the immortality symbol itself.

Almost ten years ago, I met a woman who had taken in several of her sister's children. Her sister had essentially abandoned them. My friend and her husband, a pastor, also had four or five of their own. Their decision to raise a brood of eight kids should have come with a warning label. Drugs, a teenage pregnancy, honor roll students, athletes—the children ran the gamut from your worst fear to your most impressive immortality symbol.

In an e-mail, she wrote, "With 8 kids we can see that it's not our parenting. You just help them stay alive until they grow into who they choose to be. A couple of my kids could make us win Parents of the Year. A couple of them could make people wonder about our parenting. Oh well, I have no regrets because every child deserves a loving home, whether they grow up to pass that on or not. And I have hope in God for those I still love who don't really love God and others." My guess is that her children are less immortality symbols and more living stories of God's grace.

Recently my wife and I attended the wedding of a doctor's daughter, and at the reception dinner that followed, we sat at a table with another guest, a wiry, tanned, middle-aged woman, the wife of a medical missionary. On furlough, she and her husband planned to return to Africa shortly. "It must be quite a shock to step off the plane from Africa," I said, "and walk into an American wedding." She waved her hand dismissively: "Nah, we learned long ago that when we're in Wheaton, we're in Wheaton, and when we're in Africa, we're in Africa."

I was startled at her apparent detachment from both cultures. Often those who serve the poor come to view their calling as an immortality symbol—and it becomes a virulent strain of self-righteousness, yet another face of the self. Yet I didn't sense in her any low-level resentment at consumptive American culture or sense of superiority or insecurity from serving on the front lines of poverty and war. She seemed truly detached, yet appeared attentive and engaged in what must have seemed to an African missionary like an opulent reception. What kind of spiritual wholeness allows her to commute between the Emerging and Industrialized Worlds with little or no anxiety?

Woah... So true...

Detached from the anxiety of the suburbs but engaged in life and in the suffering around her. Not absorbed into the suburban or Emerging World stream but fully alive in it. Is there a better illustration of the deeper life? I believe she is truly free. I believe she has learned "the unforced rhythms of grace," has learned "to live freely and lightly" (Matt. 11:28–30, The Message).

4

About-Face

Environmental Toxin: "I want my neighbor's life."
Spiritual Practice: Friendship with those who have no
immortality symbols

The first couple of years running my business, as with most start-ups, my small financial raft almost sank. Not all that remarkable for such poor planning. I tend to act first and then plan. There are consequences for that. A friend consoled me by saying that all our financial woes would eventually be "paragraph three in a Forbes magazine cover story." He's a politician. So far he has been wrong.

At first, I really didn't mind living on the edge. What cut most deeply, though, was what I had to drive. It annoyed me that I had to park off-site or out of sight when visiting a client. I often took the train into the city and then a cab to client offices. Once I even borrowed a car. On occasion, I rented an SUV for a couple of hours, if the client meeting involved taking him or her to lunch. I certainly couldn't show up in our rusted, four-door red Buick. My wife drove the minivan.

Early one Sunday morning, I stopped for coffee at the Latte Temple and then headed for worship band practice at church, about five minutes away. It was about 7:15 A.M., the streets sleepy and the winter light dim. Running late, I pulled up behind an SUV that cost about a fourth of the original price of our house. I realized later that I had mindlessly tailgated the vehicle all the way to the church parking lot. I pulled up beside the truck to park, and out stepped a gray-haired member of the church. "Oh, it's just you," she said. "I wondered who was following me in that 'grandma car.'"

I inhaled sharply, almost sucking in an entire latte. I mumbled something about the high personal cost of being an entrepreneur and then turned to lug into the sanctuary my Stratocaster and backpack of gear. It really was a "grandma car": it was a hand-me-down from Grandma Goetz—her "little red car," as she used to call it. Only it really wasn't little. It was more like an ocean liner, like you'd board for a cruise. I was never more emotionally free than I was the Friday afternoon that I unbolted my vanity license plates from my grandma car and rebolted them to an SUV. *My* SUV.

The church grandma had unwittingly poked a hole in my deepest insecurity. People really did notice what I drove: "Isn't it so sad that Dave and Jana have to drive that ocean liner? They are really such a nice little family."

The suburbs seem to promote a kind of vigilance on the possessions of others. It includes both a hyperconsciousness of self ("I wonder if people notice where *we* live—in a small ranch on the *north* side of Wheaton") and a hypervigilance on the possessions of others ("Hey, how can *they* afford to tear down their house and build that huge house? Who died?"). It seems to be more than just old-fashioned coveting—"God, I wish I had enough money for that sports car"—the kind the Tenth Commandment warns against. This, though, seems to be more like a permanent state of consciousness. It's a ubiquitous, heightened vigilance—roving eyes, like a sentinel—eternally on point to compare myself to those I perceive to have more than I. I'm always weighing my immortality symbols against others'.

Several years ago, a friend commented that she had had four similar but separate conversations one evening at a church gathering, all four with young mothers of second-graders. Each mentioned, separately, that she had petitioned the local elementary school to get her child into the talented and gifted (TAG) program. Apparently, none of their second-graders had scored high enough on the standardized test. Each, though, felt her second-grader deserved to be among the "Ivy League–bound" of third grade. (In our school district, second-graders take standardized tests in the second

half of the year to spot them for the third-grade TAG program.)

One mother carped that while helping out one afternoon in her son's class, she had discovered (through the colored "book bin" system) that there were three kids ahead of her sweetie—that is, reading at a higher level. She said she asked the teacher to demonstrate that the others were truly ahead of her son. When the teacher balked, the woman marched into the principal's office, demanding that he yank the records of all three kids. She had to know the truth.

In *The Sabbath,* Jewish writer Abraham Heschel points out that the Tenth Commandment, the prohibition against coveting, is the only commandment that is proclaimed twice. "Clearly it was reiterated in order to stress its extraordinary importance."[1] Exodus 20:17 says, "Do not covet your neighbor's house. Do not covet your neighbor's wife" (NLT).

Coveting may be the most toxic indulgence of the suburbs, and the life practice to overcome it requires the discipline to face another kind of person. This person is not like me. This person is not like my neighbor, whose house I covet. This person is invisible to me, because I am facing in the wrong direction—toward those I perceive to have more than I. This is the third key practice for entering suburbia's thicker life.

SYMBOL COMPETITION

The gross revenues of my suburb's Park District must dwarf the entire state budget of North Dakota. We receive the Park District quarterly catalog (about the size of *War and Peace*) of sporting opportunities and activities for our kids, it seems, at least five to six months before they occur. And if we fail to budget for all our quarterly Park District expenses, we still have our credit card; they are as important as our house payment, if not more so. If you snooze (forget to sign up your six-year-old daughter for soccer), not only do you lose, but you predestine yourself (mostly) and your children to eternal insignificance. Your kids may end up on a waiting list. Or worse, they may not get on the team with the same coach they had last year. May it never be! A colleague described her fear when her seven-year-old son dropped out of Tae Kwon Do, so that he wasn't in any Park District sport for the winter quarter: "Am I ruining his chances for all kinds of sports when he's in high school?"

TAG programs, the traveling soccer team, the freshman basketball team, the SAT score—such symbols concretely, in the here and now, confer glory, something to be worshipped by the have-nots. Surprisingly, most of us seem to feel like we're have-nots. I wish my son could win the school's essay contest, and the winner's father comments on how good my son is at baseball.

The 'burbs are all about striving to be unique, but we all end up competing for the same symbols—the four-bedroom home with the Pottery Barn colors, the L.L. Bean underwear and outerwear, the fuel-guzzling truck, the purebred dog, the family pilgrimage to Disney World, and the athletic and scholarship-bedecked college-bound freshman. My wife says she doesn't really covet her neighbor's husband but only the figure of his size 6 wife. I can live with that.

An acquaintance once confessed to me that he "covets more on Sunday morning than any other day in the week." It's the SUVs and late-model convertibles in the church parking lot, he says. He makes a decent living but works for a nonprofit organization. I overheard another say she had pulled her kids from the local conservative Christian school because she couldn't handle sitting in her minivan, idling in line with the Mercedes and BMWs when picking up her kids. I used to think that only those with "lower paying jobs" (teachers, social workers, professional Christian workers, some construction trades) felt this way, but maybe not. I once saw a medical doctor for an outpatient surgery, and by the end of my follow-up appointment, he had pitched me on his new Internet marketing scheme. "I've got friends who graduated only from college," he said, "who make way more than I do. I wonder some days if I should have gone to medical school."

I didn't think to ask my wife later if I really looked that gullible in my hospital gown.

The last times my wife Jana and I purchased a home, we decided beforehand how much we could spend. Then, in the process of securing a loan, we learned that, technically, we could afford much more than what we had agreed upon. The bigger-is-better argument made good sense: "Your income will rise, so your payments will eventually be easier to make. Plus, property is a good investment. There's a limited supply of land; it will always go up."

When the real estate agent drove us around to look at homes, I read between the lines: "You don't want to buy in this neighborhood"—meaning, "You can afford more, move up a level." A volcano of insecurity began to erupt: *We'll never get a house we really like. I need to make more money.* It hurts when you can't buy the house you think you need.

Why do I feel as if I'll never have *enough*? Why am I oblivious to much of what I have—except that which is just out of reach? I hesitate to call this chronic emotional state *evil,* because doing so feels like vitiating the horrible atrocities that play out on the world stage each day. But could it be? Could this obsession with the good life just out of my grasp be a covert manifestation of evil in my life?

Good

Who will ask me the real questions: "Will buying this house honor God? Will it give you a sense of peace? Or will it add to your stress?" A man in his mid-forties, who made millions earlier in life, put it this way: "I knew a guy who I *knew* was making less than I but living in a nicer house. I couldn't let that happen. And so my wife and I built a bigger house." That sounds an awful lot like the man in Jesus' parable who kept building bigger barns.

CRAVING COMAS

Mountain climbers often experience HACE (high-altitude cerebral edema), which can put them into a drunken state because of a lack of oxygen. HACE can strike without warning. The brain swells, and "as pressure builds inside the skull, motor and mental skills deteriorate with alarming speed—typically within a few hours or less—and often without the victim even noticing the change."[2] The person lapses into a coma and may die if he or she is not shuttled to a lower altitude. The competitive environment of the suburbs tends to disable, with time, even the most genuine promise to live with the humility, service, and contentment God wants from us. And often without the victim noticing the change.

A pastor told me about his resentment at seeing a college friend succeed in business and then reap an affluent lifestyle. The reverend said he felt left behind. His decision to preach the gospel (in an affluent community) meant no luxury SUV or second home in Beaver Creek, present or future. It was as if he awakened in midlife, like Rip Van Winkle, and realized he had been wrong all along: this life really is all there is.

In Exodus 20:17, the Hebrew term for "covet" is *hamed,* which means "desire, take pleasure in," and the word is used both negatively and positively in the Bible.[3] The word *crave* captures the darker side of the Tenth Commandment. I *crave* carbohydrates, sugar, caffeine, salt—when I attempt to diet. And it's never a one-time impulse. It's a state of craving, which doesn't go away quickly unless I satisfy it, and doesn't stay away easily, unless a greater vision beckons ("I'm 165 pounds and full of energy").

No doubt our twenty-four-hour streaming advertising culture nourishes the cravings for my neighbor's better life. Even our elementary schools can't escape it. Today corporations hire agencies to sponsor field trips for elementary students—but not to visit Chicago's Shedd Aquarium or kick over rocks for nymphs in the local stream. Kids "study retail" at high-end sports stores. Students leave with a tote bag branded with the company logo. The school district gets cheap field trips. And no one gets hurt, right?[4]

Many are the tips for coping with a consumerist culture. You can turn off or throw away your television, limit your Christmas spending (the $100 Christmas), buy your kids clothes at the annual resale fair, buy your own espresso machine and concoct your cappuccinos at home, or drive your grandma's car during a business start-up—the how-to list is infinite. Pick up the *Utne Reader* or any other alternative magazine, you'll find all sorts of mostly helpful advice.

A few, to escape from the environmental pressure, flee the suburbs for the country, much like a few early church fathers headed for the desert. Doing so can't hurt. The nagging problem is, of course, that you can take yourself out of the world, to state the familiar truth, but you can't take the world out of yourself. My parents chose to take me out of the world, shipping me off to a fundamentalist co-ed high school on the prairies of South Dakota. At fourteen, I lived like a college student, housed in a dorm with others my age. And mind you, the girls' dorm was not a direct shot from the boys'. The school was so separatist it was located thirteen miles from the nearest town (virtually assuring no contamination from the world), which had less than a couple thousand inhabitants. School rules locked down all aspects of your life. For example, "the six-inch rule": if you had a girlfriend, at all times you had to be at least six inches from her. We students worked out, secretly, a new way of measuring that: from your tonsils to hers. Rules were an aphrodisiac.

Ha!

You can take the coveter out of the 'burb, but you can't take the craving out of the coveter.

ESCAPE FROM ALCATRAZ

How do I escape from the cravings of my gluttonous, overindulged self?

How do I free myself from the invisible Alcatraz of the suburbs? There's no greater bondage than living only for what I don't yet have and for the evasive approval of people who, frankly, I don't really know or care about and who will always have just a little more than I. There's a reason why covetousness made the top ten. Abraham Heschel writes that "inner liberty depends upon being exempt from domination of things as well as domination of people."[5] I am not free if the essence of my vision for life is "Supersize it" or "I'll have the 'extra value' house." I am in maximum security, locked down, with no hope of parole.

So where's the free and light life that Christ supposedly offers me?

The answer seems to be the same as for most questions of spirituality: there's no straight shot from here to there. There's no how-to tip for a conscience and lifestyle free from cravings for your neighbor's wife and kids—or the appearance of his seemingly perfect life. [Read a magazine article for tighter abs, but not to transform your reality.] A soul practice is, over a lifetime, a means of opening ourselves up to a reality that is larger and truer than our own. The witness from much of Christian history is unanimous: "The freer you are from exerting your own effort, the more quickly you will move toward your Lord."[6] It's counterintuitive—crazy, really. If I can start a business, why can't I simply *will* my way out of this one? I'll just try harder, right?

In *Mission in Christ's Way,* Lesslie Newbigin, a twentieth-century Anglican missionary to India, describes the time when he, as a religious dignitary, visited a village in the Madras diocese. There were two entrances to the village—the north side and the south side—and the only way to get to the village was by crossing a river. The congregation collected at the south side of the village to welcome Newbigin. "They had prepared a welcome such as only an Indian village can prepare," writes Newbigin. "There was music and fireworks and garlands and fruit . . . everything you can imagine." By accident, he arrived at the north end, where only a few goats and chickens greeted him. Newbigin writes, "I had to disappear while word was sent to the assembled congregation, and the entire village did a sort of U-turn so as to face the other direction. Then I duly appeared."[7]

The U-turn, says Newbigin, is the notion behind the New Testament Greek term *metanoia*, "repent." The spiritual U-turn is an about-face, which is the first step toward freedom from an obsession with my neighbor's good life. To face the opposite direction is to face the humanity of another kind of person. Instead of riveting my gaze on the possessions of others economically above me, I do an about-face. I turn to face the person whom I perceive to have less than I. This suburban life practice is all about finding ways to be with the poor, the mentally disabled, the old and alone, the depressed, the spiritually broken— essentially, all those who don't build up my ego through their presence. This practice, though, is not really about helping those folks. It's really about helping ourselves; it's the sure entrance into the thicker world. A friend, a social worker who assists elderly abused by their kids, has a card taped above her desk: "People with mental illnesses enrich our lives." This quasi-spiritual discipline is, over a lifetime, about opening ourselves up to the people in and with whom God seems to be most active. Wow

Frankly, it seems patronizing even to use the phrase "those with less than I," because I then become the judge of what constitutes normal. As someone who spends more on a venti-decaf-hazelnut-extra-hot latte than much of the world makes in an entire day, I have little to say about what's normal.

THE EMPTYING DISCIPLINE

In her *New York Times* bestseller, *Nickel and Dimed,* social critic Barbara Ehrenreich narrates the funny, poignant, and downright depressing stories found during her undercover assignment as a low-income wage earner. No spring chicken, Ehrenreich set out to see what it was like to try to make a living on $6 or $7 an hour. At the tail end of the dot-com era (the late 1990s), when the soaring U.S. economy was still in denial, she worked as a waitress in Key West, Florida, then as a Merry Maid and a nursing home assistant in Maine, and finally as a Wal-Mart associate in the Twin Cities area in Minnesota. I'm sure Ms. Ehrenreich, a self-described atheist, would not appreciate the comparison, but as I read of her experience, I couldn't help but think of the Christian doctrine of kenosis. Kenosis ("emptying") is the theological attempt to explain what happened when God became a human in the person of Jesus: he voluntarily gave up all his regality and nobility and power as God to enter the world as a baby.

For basically a magazine article (and eventually a book), Ehrenreich, a Ph.D. in biology, voluntarily gave up her rights as an overly educated upper-middle-class journalist. She emptied herself (kenosis) of her status to experience what almost 30 percent of the American workforce endures: trying to make ends meet on less than $8 an hour.[8] She struggles to find affordable housing, tries to balance two physically exhausting jobs, and negotiates in humiliation for food stamps. While in Maine, she writes in her journal, "MESSAGE TO ME FROM MY FORMER SELF: SLOW DOWN AND, ABOVE ALL, DETACH. If you can't stand being around suffering people, then you have no business in the low-wage work world, as a journalist or anything else."[9]

But Ehrenreich could not detach. She feels compassion for Holly, the pregnant twenty-three-year-old Merry Maids team leader who fears telling her husband the news and whose lunch each day amounts to a bag of Doritos. It appears that Holly can't afford much more than Doritos. And then Ehrenreich gets angry. She steps in to assist Holly when the mom-to-be apparently breaks her foot while cleaning. Ehrenreich's heroics lead nowhere. Holly really doesn't want help. But that, really, is beside the point.

The point—the soul practice—is Ehrenreich's kenosis. The practice is endemic to who God is: emptying yourself of power and refraining from doing in life only that which feeds your ego (frenetically worrying about getting your student in the TAG program, for example) to live among and learn from the powerless. There's little, however, in my suburban experience, as pietistic as my community is, that encourages kenosis. Not even in my religious community: I am encouraged to read my Bible more ("Get in the Word"). I am cajoled to serve on a church committee ("The leadership team really needs your gifts this year"). I never feel as if I share my faith enough ("Don't you care that millions are dying without Christ?"). I'm told that I really need to join a small group ("You need to find a safe place where you can be vulnerable."). And when Jana and I do join one, we're careful to choose a group with some "key couples in the church."

I'm sure my church challenges its members to serve those who are different than us. Perhaps I hear that message, though, only as a program. It's just so much easier to sign up for another year on the spiritual formation committee than it is to find time to be with the *only* people who can help me enter the kingdom of God. Recently, our church supported a refugee family from Africa as it resettled in our community. Many spent untold hours helping the family (which included a husband, one of his three wives, four of his nineteen children, and one granddaughter) set up an apartment nearby. The family needed a television to learn English, so my wife purchased one at a good price, and the new television sat, boxed, in our living room for about two weeks. I wanted my oldest, Christian, to drop off the television with me, to see up close what apartment living is like. But although the apartment was a mere four blocks away, I simply couldn't find the time to get both of us over there. One cold and windy Sunday afternoon in March, we finally made the delivery, and I had a funny conversation with one of the older sons, who asked, in broken English, about cable. They had been in the States for only six weeks. I told him that it cost money for cable, but that with the rabbit ears he could get at least five channels. He wasn't impressed.

Later I realized why the television had sat in our living room for two weeks: I feared what might happen when I made contact with the refugees. The gift might create a relationship.

SIN WITH AND SIN FOR

A couple I know who can only be described as upper-middle-class models the life practice of kenosis as well as anyone. He's an executive with a Fortune 500 company, and she a writer for a local newspaper and a mom to three. In the late eighties, before having kids, Kirk and Sherry lived in Eastern Europe for twelve months while he completed some fieldwork at a rural "institute" while working on a Ph.D. in economics from a Big Ten university. They lived on love and borscht in a rural village. For the locals of the region, though, food was scarce, their rubles worthless. "March was an especially dreary month—muddy, chilly," Sherry says, "and by then families had depleted all their home-canned goods. Their diets consisted mainly of stale bread, chunks of seasoned beef fat, and soggy potatoes."

One predictably dreary spring day, Sherry opened her door to a young woman and her father, who had dropped by to introduce themselves. "There they stood," says Sherry, "with their last jars of precious canned tomatoes from their home stash." When Kirk and Sherry left the village a year later, they were leaving friends: "If you're ever in the States, please look us up!" I've said that same line before as I've waved good-bye to new friends after a short-term mission trip. I didn't *really* mean it.

One afternoon years later, the phone rang, and Kirk and Sherry's second son, Andrew, picked it up: "Mom, there's this crazy lady on the phone." It was the young woman who had offered Sherry her last canned tomatoes: "We found you, we found you!" she said in her broken English.

The upshot was that the young woman (who was now not as young) and a friend were not in the States only for a week or two. Their visit was permanent. Sherry says, "I must admit, it was a little frightening at first. How could we possibly find the time or the energy for anyone else in our busy life? Were they penniless? What did they want from us? And finally I asked myself, 'Why me?'"

But the relationships picked up where they had left off. "I was reminded of their gentleness," she says, "and I saw their desperate desire to have a better life. I was reminded of the day they gave to us all they had left." The two arrived like most immigrants: with nothing except hope for an honest living. Sherry got the word out to her church, and the two women received bedding, used furniture, and a little cash for the transition. But Sherry didn't ditch the relationships once the crisis passed, though I'm sure the thought must have crossed her mind. For a woman with three elementary-age sports-minded kids, that could have been easily justified. But Sherry persuaded her upper-middle-class friends to begin using the home cleaning service these two women had started, essentially launching them into their own business. Recently one of the women married, but both still work in the business.

Sherry says, "It has not always been easy. But once I

took that step forward, God took over." Kirk and Sherry recently moved out of state, but the friendships continue through calls, e-mail, letters, and occasional visits.

Martin Luther, the sixteenth-century religious curmudgeon and reformer who triggered one of the avalanches that shook Christendom, believed that "the Christian man [and woman, of course] is so to identify himself with his neighbor as to take to himself sins that he has not personally committed."[10] Luther scoffed at the notion of trying to keep "the record clean. The Christian, like Christ, must in some sense become sin with and for the sinner."[11]

I take Luther to mean: forget trying to live a safe, gated life. Religion isn't about your piety, it's about loving your neighbor (not his house). And it isn't about heroics— trying to make a *difference* with your life by moving to Bangladesh. It starts with a simple awakening to the suffering around you. It opens you up to a world that is more rich and reflective of the heart of God.

Kenosis may be the spiritual practice that comes closest to satisfying my deepest craving: an inner liberation from the domination of what others think and what others have. I know I should be more grateful when I covet my neighbor's Jamaican spring break vacation, but when

I walk into the apartment of a refugee family and smell the damp, stale air and see their eager countenance, I begin to compare myself to a different kind of neighbor. And then it just happens: I begin to experience gratitude, which is one of the primary emotions found in the thicker world.

Remembering Laughter

Environmental Toxin: "My life should be easier than it is."
Spiritual Practice: Accepting my cross with grace and patience

W hile working as a magazine editor, I was assigned to interview Joni, a woman who had become a quadriplegic as a teenager after diving into a lake. Almost thirty years had passed, and this woman's achievements as a book author, artist, songwriter, advocate for the disabled, and public speaker were astounding.

I had flown from Chicago to California; the pressure was on to deliver a solid interview for the magazine. I arrived early and was ushered into a small studio like that of an artist. One of her beautiful paintings sat atop an easel. After a short delay, Joni Eareckson Tada was wheeled into the room by her assistant. The interviewee, now in midlife, apologized for being late, and I introduced myself, thanking her for granting the interview, and as I did so, I picked up a magazine copy that I had brought along and thoughtlessly handed it to her to view.

"I'm a *quad*riplegic," she said. "I can't hold the magazine. You can put it on the desk." I almost went into anaphylactic shock, my mind freezing in humiliation, a deep embarrassment coursing through my soul. What was I thinking? I knew that she couldn't hold the magazine. "Uh, sorry."

This interview is over before it has begun, I thought. *She won't continue after this stupid blunder.* Isn't it strange that in a moment when I had been so rude I could think only of what the insult would do for *my* needs?

Minutes later, her assistant brought in coffee for both of us and then left the room. "Can you help me take a sip of my coffee?" my interviewee asked. "Sure," I said. "I don't want to spill it on you. I've never done this before." I stood up and picked up the cup. Never since have I felt as insecure: I put the cup to her lips and lifted it ever so slowly so not to scald her lips and chin or spill it down the front of her. In her simple, gracious request, it was as if she were saying, "Dave, you've made a bonehead mistake. I'm going to illustrate to you how much I need you. I am so disabled that I need you even to help me drink my coffee."

During the next forty-five minutes, she opened up about her fears of growing old and what that might mean for her creativity. We discussed the meaning of suffering, and I'll never forget how rattled I felt near the beginning of the interview when she made an almost offhand comment: "I think life is supposed to be hard." I'm still arguing with that in my head, a decade or more later.

But what shook me most was her gracious response to my stupid blunder. I still marvel at how someone who has suffered so much could act so loving to a stranger. I felt I deserved to be drop-kicked off the top floor of the building. Instead, she gave me an extra fifteen minutes of her time; the interview ran longer than either of us planned. What prompts such a generous spirit amid such suffering?

I can't say for sure, but I think Joni has come to terms with the suffering in her life. At some point, she stopped fighting against it. She had to. You don't exude that kind of graciousness by denial. My guess is that every morning Joni has to re-up. She has to stop fighting what she cannot change.

I have a cross, you have a cross, Joni has a cross. The size and weight are not even across the board. My neighbor gets one kind of suffering, I get another. Suffering isn't meted out evenhandedly. One Christian theme throughout the centuries is a sort of making peace or coming to terms with one's allotment of suffering. It's not an abstract theological issue about whether a God that's good can be culpable for what is bad in this world. It's existential. It's personal: is my God good when my life isn't (or doesn't feel good)?

I struggle to write about my cross on Ranch Road, where hard times mean, mostly, road construction on

Main Street. But even in my isolation ward, where I scrub feverishly to kill off all the bacteria on the unit called my life, there's no immunity from it. I want the thicker life in Christ, but I often don't want to address the hard reality of my life. This fourth spiritual practice is not so much something to do as something to stop doing, to accept the life I've been given. Even in suburbia, life is hard.

ENVIRONMENTAL CHARACTER

In *The Ends of the Earth,* travel journalist Robert Kaplan reflected on life in Iran after the revolution that overthrew the shah in the late 1970s. "As public life had been circumscribed," he writes, "I observed that ... private life here had become richer in order to compensate."[1] As the new militant government created intense economic and social pressure, as the struggle simply to exist became more fierce, the home life of Iranians deepened.

No doubt the environmental component of physical struggle creates character and a richness and texture of soul. With less physical discomfort, character forms differently, if not more slowly. Saints may be harder to make on Ranch Road. Environmental suffering (persecution for your faith or the lack of basic necessities of life, for example), which has conscripted many into sainthood for a couple thousand years of Christian history, has been all but eradicated, at least for the middle and upper middle classes.

I grew up in a home where foreign missionary work was elevated as the ultimate sacrifice for Christ. I came to understand the word *suffering* primarily in one narrow sense: the noble or heroic suffering that comes at the hands of persecutors, such as the suffering of Christ or of the apostle Paul, Christianity's dominant missionary in the first century. Or that of believers who die in steamy Amazon jungles at the hands of restless natives. The word *suffering* was used largely in the context of some great personal sacrifice for or because of Christ.

If you're part of the Christian minority in a Muslim or Hindu community, you might see suffering primarily as prejudice or persecution, and for good reason. But that sense of suffering is only one section of a much larger frame of meaning, while taking nothing away from the persecuted saints of church history and in our time.

Pure and simple, life is supposed to be hard, to borrow Joni's line, even on Ranch Road. The patently obvious needs to be stated: suffering in the 'burbs is not suffering in the Emerging World. It's easy, though, to mock the chai-latte angst of my quiet community, where an acquaintance hovers over even the poop schedules of her four boys under nine. But no matter how many environmental contributors to human suffering get managed into obsolescence, the good life is not contiguous. It ends badly for everyone.

A colleague once commented in passing that she could never fully sympathize with the hard times of some of her friends: divorce, financial stress, special needs children, job loss. Her life was a Cinderella story, the part after she meets her prince. She made the comment to me shortly before her world collapsed. She was in her early sixties, and within a two-year span, her husband *and* her eighty-four-year-old mother were diagnosed with cancer. She was a strong person, a beam of support through their radiation and chemotherapy. Then she herself was diagnosed with cancer and died within four months, her husband and mother outliving her.

My father recalls that when he was ten, near the end of World War II, he looked up from his play and saw black smoke rising in the dry, hot July afternoon from the prairie farm of his uncle and aunt, about a quarter mile away. My dad's thirteen-year-old cousin had been ironing and had fallen asleep on the couch. Apparently the windows were open, and curtains on the wall by the kerosene stove used to heat the iron caught fire. Within a flash, with the hot wind, the flames licked up the walls, the house engulfed in flames and smoke. The girl's mother, my great aunt Katie, was at work in the harvest, windrowing wheat a few miles away. The girl's father was at work on the other side of the barn—say, seventy-five yards from the house—putting new siding on a granary, which would store the grain from the harvest. His back was turned to the house, and by the time he noticed the black plume, his daughter and house were ashes.

A friend's forty-year-old brother collapsed in a Foot Locker store, the news gutting her life. She lived the dream: three beautiful, well-adjusted kids, a sprawling house in a new subdivision, a husband on the corporate dole. Weeks later, after the funeral, one of her friends brought over some photos of a peaceful early winter afternoon. The photos pictured her children, happy, bundled, joyful. She looked at the date on the photos. The time was the exact moment her brother had died—although she didn't know it, of course, when the photos were being snapped. The call came several hours later. Later she commented, "While my life was merrily happening, it was also changing, in ways I could never imagine."

That is the true nature of life; we try to control it and in the process it controls us, picking us up randomly, like a tornado, and dropping us into a foreign place. Writer Kurt Vonnegut once said, "Don't worry about the future. Or worry, but know that worrying is as effective as trying to solve an algebra problem by chewing bubble gum. The real troubles in your life are apt to be things that never crossed your mind, the kind that blindside you at 4 P.M. on some idle Tuesday."[2]

MY CROSS, YOUR CROSS

As life picks up speed and as I clock more days and weeks and years, I accumulate more suffering. The human tendency seems to be to fight the difficult parts of life, as if by resisting them I can skip to the good stuff or set a few extra goals to overcome the suffering. Isn't the deeper spiritual life supposed to be more satisfying, more connected, more peaceful?

A therapist in the Chicago western suburbs once told me that in her practice she sees quite a few angry early adolescent kids. I asked her what makes them angry. "Mothers who love too much."

She gave the example of a young mother who puts away the paint set and cleans up the mess for her child because he has moved on to play with something else. But twenty minutes later, when the child begs his mother to paint again, instead of saying, "Sorry, I already put it all away; find something else to do," the mother drags out the paints again. Over time, the therapist thinks, such overparenting sets some kids up for a more difficult journey through adolescence. As small disappointments at school or in the home begin to collect, anger pools and then floods their life. It isn't fair!

No one really sets out to think this way: that the good life is within reach, and if I'm not experiencing it, then all I need to do is work harder to make it happen. It must be the caffeine in my lattes. In *Beginning to Pray,* Eastern Orthodox archbishop Anthony Bloom writes, "We all assume that we are deep and that the deeper we go, the more delightful it will be."[3] That's orthodox suburban thinking. But it's also spiritual heresy. There's no entrance into the thicker reality of Christ's presence without the cross. No one has to go looking for one; the cross finds you. I've got bigger problems than a baseball coach who won't let my son pitch.

I once spoke at a weekend retreat for suburban men, and five minutes into the first session on Friday evening, I was already taking on water. My subject matter was the crisis of limits that many men face in midlife or beyond, but I may as well have been lecturing on differential equations. There was no resonance. Fifty deadpan faces—professors, entrepreneurs, bankers, and plumbers—stared back at me. Decent guys all, they even tried consoling me during the break. A man in his late thirties with a Ph.D. in engineering said, "Dave, I think I can help you understand what you're saying." Then he drew a graph for me on a napkin.

I should have chosen a sexier topic, like coming to terms with your father wound or understanding the Christian male within. I was struck by the group's optimism. I'm paraphrasing at this juncture, but their comments on suffering essentially were: your troubles in life simply create an opportunity to buck up and find a way through them, and no matter what happens, God always has something better for you, he has a plan. That's the kind of positive thinking you'd expect from the white male hegemony. Franciscan Richard Rohr argues that the primary spiritual journey for men in the second half of life is descent, the way of the cross, giving up power. If you want to be a sweet grandfather and not a bitter old man, then you must learn how to embrace suffering. No wonder the retreat went so poorly. The "journey of descent" is a hard sell to those in power.

In contrast, I've always been intrigued by how parents with a special needs child rethink their dreams in a culture that deifies the unlimited potential of children, one immortality symbol. Such parents know limits. You can't "positive-think" your way out of a special needs child. Adjusting life's expectations to serve a child with disabilities, when the other mothers in your book club whine about whether the classroom teacher is properly groom-

Good

ing their gifted child, can be disheartening. It's hard to believe that God has something better for your child when you fear the time when he can't be mainstreamed anymore. What will happen to his friends if he has to go to a special school?

I watched my grandparents live out their golden years with a mentally disabled son who was finally emancipated at sixty-five when my ninety-one-year-old grandmother moved in with her only daughter. My grandfather died without seeing his middle child live on his own. I grew up cringing at (and mimicking) my uncle's occasional quirky behavior. Even to this day, when I'm with him in public, I instinctively turn to see if anyone is watching. I'm sure my uncle, who appears to have limited reasoning abilities, must know deep in his soul that his family struggled to honor him as a full human being.

A friend describes the intensity of accepting the disability of one of their six children: "Early on, Jill and I were consumed with our son's disability as we tried to determine what we were dealing with and how to best meet his needs. It was a day-to-day struggle that took a toll on our family in all dimensions (mental, physical, relational, emotional, and spiritual)."

Many families don't make it; the divorce rate spikes among couples with special needs kids. My friend and his wife agonized over whether to continue the endless testing and analysis. Was it really autism? The alternative was to accept their son's condition and move on to managing their growing family as a whole. "The all-consuming quest," he said, "for that elusive 'fix' was damaging to, perhaps would have even destroyed, our family."

They finally stopped the pursuit.

"We started viewing and treating Jonathon as our son rather than our 'autistic child,'" he says. "We have expectations of him like we do the rest of our kids: He shares a room with his little brother, he has to put his dishes away, he takes the bus to school, he walks the dog, he gets in trouble when he breaks a rule. . . . He just happens to be autistic." WOW. . .

The challenges of raising an autistic child don't evaporate, of course, just because you choose not to obsess about it: "Jonathon's disability has been, is, and always will be a part of our daily family life," his father says, "but we choose not to allow his disability to consume us and define us as a family. His needs are not our family focus." I asked him how Jonathon's disability affected my friend's relationship with God in recent years, and he wrote me in an e-mail "God essentially said, 'My grace is sufficient for you.' In other words, 'Deal with it.'"

"Dealing with it" is not another technique for the spiritually sated to add to their repertoire of spiritual retreats, spiritual directors, and weekends at a wooded

monastery. Perhaps the word is "relinquishing" or "surrendering" or "abandoning." All sound like cliches, given
my religious community's thirst for all things spiritually
chic. (Right now, all things "ancient" are *in*.) This is not
really so much a spiritual practice as it is a discovery or an
insight. And it's not a one-time discovery but a continual
discovering. These are not sentimental moments, when
deep feelings of Christ's presence lift me into ecstasy
while I gaze at the Milky Way galaxy; they are, first, ex-
hausting moments, when I stop my mental efforts to
concoct a scheme to throw off my cross. And then, perhaps, comes for the first time a modicum of God's presence or peace. It's where for the first time I begin to see
all things as coming from the hand of God, even, or especially, the cross itself.

"To penetrate deeper in the experience of Jesus
Christ," writes Jeanne Guyon, a sixteenth-century Christian mystic, "it is required that you begin to abandon
your whole existence.... You must utterly believe that
the circumstances of your life, that is, every minute of
your life, as well as the whole course of your life ... have
all come to you by His will and by His permission."[4]

FREEDOM OF OBEDIENCE

The free and light life of Christ often begins, truly, on the far side of abandonment—after I stop fighting the suffering that God has allowed into my life. Eastern Orthodox archbishop Anthony Bloom writes, "When we have come to a certain depth, it is all right, but on the way it looks very much like the quest of the Grail."[5] Perhaps the Holy Grail itself is accepting that "the faithful Giver of every good gift gives the cross to you with his own hand."[6]

Mature Christian faith discerns God behind _all_ the circumstances in life that conceal God—from the mundane to the tragic. Such understanding is not the domain of detached theologians, with no skin in the game, who argue the theology of God's goodness. No, these may be the most terrifying moments, when I begin to love God for God and not only for the gifts of God. Would I love God if I didn't live the good life on Ranch Road? I don't know.

In a 1942 letter to his twin sister, Sabine, Dietrich Bonhoeffer, who was later hanged by the Nazis, wrote:

READ

It is good to learn early enough that suffering and God are not a contradiction but rather a unity, for the idea that God himself is suffering is one that has always been one of the most convincing teachings of Christianity. I think <u>God is nearer to</u> <u>suffering</u> than to happiness, and to find God in this way gives peace and rest and a strong and courageous heart.[7]

wow.

I wish Bonhoeffer were wrong, but there seems to be no other road to a deeper sense of God's peace. I risk the embittered journey the more I hedge against suffering or bargain with God to get out of my troubles in the easiest, most comfortable way.

Remembering Laughter, a novel by Wallace Stegner, chronicles the suffering brought about by an affair. Alec Stuart is a wealthy Iowa farmer, and he and his wife, Margaret, have a comfortable, if not intimate, marriage until a few months after her sister, Elspeth, arrives from Scotland to live with them. Alec ends up doing the un-thinkable (or at least untenable): he sleeps with his wife's younger sister. Alec and Elspeth's affair triggers a heart-breaking set of consequences, including an illegitimate son named Malcolm. In a strange twist, Elspeth stays on the farm with her child, and Malcolm grows up in the farmhouse with the three, not knowing that Elspeth is his real mother or that Alec is his father. Alec, Elspeth, and Margaret, in a conspiracy of silence, agree to raise Malcolm as if he were an adopted member of the family. For years, Margaret wields power in the family as the victim, never releasing her bitterness or absolving her sister and husband of their shame. I can't say I blame her.

Malcolm grows up calling his father "Uncle Alec." The only warmth in this tragedy is the relationship between Alec and Malcolm, who, of course, are in reality father and son. Amid the bitterness and regret, Alec figures out how to "remember laughter" as he plays with his son out of sight in the farmyard, away from the two women.

The real danger on Ranch Road, then, is not the suffering itself—your husband sleeping with your sister—but missing out on the joy in life after he does. To remember laughter may mean first being willing to carry my cross, what God has entrusted to me for this life. That can happen only after the fighting stops, after I abandon my attempts to live a life other than my own.

So much of coveting seems to originate from a deep dissatisfaction with the life I've been given. I want my neighbor's life. It's strange, really, to hate the life I have, since I've made sure that every step along the way has been chosen by me. I choose that college, I choose this spouse, I choose my wedding gifts, I choose to go back and get an MBA, I choose when to have kids, I choose to buy in this neighborhood. And yet, in many ways, I still fight the life I think I've chosen.

I can't say for sure that one family somewhere doesn't live the perfect suburban life with just the right number of immortality symbols and no suffering. I hope that family exists, if only to give me hope. The only problem with that thinking is that, of course, it's not based on any relationship with them. [If I knew them as human beings, I'd discover that not all is as it appears. Perception is not only *not* reality, it's also dehumanizing. Sooner or later, each person's life runs out of its ten thousand joys, and then comes the suffering: the unexpected fourth child with Down syndrome, ten years of paying either the rent or your daughter's ballet fees after the divorce, the dive into the lake that causes quadriplegia. And then what?]

In the mid-nineties, I struck up a friendship with an Episcopalian priest while editing an article he wrote about the death of his son. It has now been more than fifteen years since his seven-year-old died of leukemia. Nicholas was buried Tuesday of Holy Week. Al and I find time for lunch a couple of times a year, and one of those times, strangely, often comes during Lent.

In a piece that Al wrote, he described the evening of Easter Sunday, days after he and his wife, Vickie, buried their oldest. He and Vickie sat on their front walk, watching the sunset and their two-year-old daughter, Hannah, who was playing in the yard.

"What do you think Nicholas sees?" Al asked his wife. "Do you think he sees this sunset?"

"He sees an even more beautiful sunset than we can see," Vickie replied.

Al, the priest, paused and then said, "What if this is all there is? What if dead is dead is dead? What if life does come to an end? What if Nick is no more?"

After a lengthy silence, Vickie said that he might be right, but that "I choose to live my life believing it is true."[8]

The priest says about six months later he chose to believe the same; the other options were not pretty: bitterness, hopelessness, isolation. Not long ago, Al told me that before his son's death, he saw life in black and white; now, many years later, he sees it in full color. I take that to mean he can laugh again, that he has remembered how to laugh again, and that not only does he see life for what it really is—one part suffering—but he can also enjoy its sweetness.

Shirker Service

Environmental Toxin: "I need to make a difference
with my life."

Spiritual Practice: Pursuing action, not results

I grew up driving behind old pickup trucks with gun racks and Cold War redneck bumper stickers that read *Ruck Fussia.* For a stretch during my high school years, I thought that for a career I'd take over my grandfather's farm. Grandpa always groaned when I mentioned the idea: "Ah, David, I don't wish that on you." I've caught on worms and minnows my share of striper bass and crappies and walleye and northern pike, and, of course, bullheads. I worked a bit on my boorish proclivities when I moved to the 'burbs, though I've resisted becoming a vegetarian. I now release most all the trout I catch (I've converted to the more palatable fly-fishing).

Only the mailperson knows I still secretly read *North Dakota Outdoors,* published by the North Dakota Game and Fish Department. The quarterly magazine recently reprinted an interview with Valerius Geist, considered one of the world's leading cervid (deer family) biologists.

A curmudgeon in the fall of life, he loves to rail against the idea of rich who can pay for "staged hunts" for deer and elk; he believes passionately in the "North American system of democratic hunting," where Joe and Jane Hunter can enjoy the great outdoors.[1]

Geist originated the "shirker bull" concept. His thesis, apparently, has stirred up his fellow wildlife scientists. The shirker bull is a male elk that is able to grow very large antlers because it "shirks his biological duty by choosing not to participate in the rut."[2] The rut is the annual fall ritual when deer and elk males square off against one another to determine sexual dominance and sire the next generation. The shirker bull, most likely a loner, avoids fighting other males and thus pours all his caloric energy into "growing exceptionally large antlers."[3]

Geist's controversial thesis is that most of the world-record antler trophies came from shirkers. That is, the really large antlered deer and elk that end up as stuffed heads in a Montana lodge were likely loners, shirking their biological duty.

In the suburban wild, Shirkers are religious folk who inadvertently disengage from the suffering of the world and who unwittingly collect to themselves every available religious experience. Whether the latest book or Bible study or spiritual director or new church with the really authentic and post-postmodern worship, Shirkers are always on the move for the next spiritual plane. Shirkers are wild for the ideas of God.

One sure sign of a Shirker is his or her relentless, unreflective pursuit of significance: I want to make a difference with my life. I want to make my life count. I want more from my life than investment banking. I'm weary of making money; I want to help poor people become suburbanites just like I am. I want to go on a mission trip and give money to help train church leaders worldwide.

Such sentiments often emerge in midlife. While the emotion is normal and healthy in the Christian young ("I want my life to make a difference for Christ"), it can be, for those religiously sated, a sign of the inverse cripple with a bloated, tiny soul. The problem isn't with the act of service but with its motivation. The fifth key spiritual practice is to move from the pursuit of significance in your life to simple obedience to the things of God. One feeds the self, the other starves it. One promises self-fulfillment, the other actually delivers it, but not in the way you expect.

MAXIMUM SECURITY SIGNIFICANCE

"Turn your head!"

"Now the other way. Open your mouth! Lift up your tongue!"

On his way to my ankles, the correctional officer brushed his hands across my crotch and patted my pants pocket.

"What's this?"

"Just my car keys."

"Only one key is permitted into the prison. You'll have to put it into a locker. To the receiving room."

I backtracked through the metal detector, secured a locker, and awaited my turn. Nearby a frail, brown-eyed elementary-aged girl and her mother also tolerated the shake down. They seemed to know the ritual: they quietly removed their shoes, moved slowly through the metal detector, and had their bodies searched by a guard of the same gender. This was more than a decade before 9/11, which made the prison-search standard at airports.

We then stood by in a small room for an old repainted school bus to ferry us the last half mile to the inmates at the Colorado maximum security prison. My guess is that the girl was visiting her father. I was visiting for the first time an inmate assigned to me by a nonprofit organization formed to help slow the escalating recidivism, or return to prison, rate. In Illinois, the recidivism rate exceeds 50 percent.[4] That is, within three years of being released, more than 50 percent of prisoners end up violating parole or committing another crime, ending up back on the government dole in prison.

I had signed up to visit an inmate once a month for one year prior to his release. The idea was that if inmates about to be released just had a friend to help them through the transition, they'd be less likely to get sent back upriver. In Colorado at the time, for most released inmates, the only reentry preparation was a bus ticket, $100 in cash, and a "Ya'll don't come back here now, ya hear?"

I don't remember why I signed up for the gig. And I really questioned my decision to do so the moment I met Perry for the first time, though I was really glad that at least he was shorter and thinner than I. I am a white Anglo-Saxon Protestant; Perry an African American agnostic. I had feared my assignment would be a three-hundred-pound inmate with a deep voice and a thing for short white boys.

"So you're the preacher," Perry mumbled. I was working at the time as a student pastor while also doing freelance writing.

"My brother's a preacher," he said. "How 'bout a pop? I'll buy you a pop."

He reached into his olive-colored prison habit and pulled out two tokens for two sodas. We retired to a corner table in the visitation room. There's nothing like the industrial warmth of harsh florescent lighting with white tile flooring and off-white walls. Children and women and elderly couples jammed the tables in the room, chatting or playing cards with their imprisoned boyfriends, husbands, and fathers. In one corner a young couple caressed each other. This would not be a conjugal visit; the guards, standing throughout the room, eyed them suspiciously.

According to Perry, I was his second visitor in three years. Even his girlfriend and son kept their distance. Perry hoped to see them soon, though; his case manager promised him freedom by spring. It was early fall, the aspens had already changed in the high country.

Perry and I usually spent about an hour and a half together. For the first couple of visits, the time dragged on like an awkward high school date. But over the next several months, with sodas and microwaved popcorn, we managed to jabber about everything from my love of fishing to his philosophy about marriage. I kept joking with Perry that he should marry his girlfriend, that if he needed my pastoral services, I'd be glad to oblige. He always replied, "Don't be tying me down, Dave."

I dreaded the trip to the correctional facility in Canon City, Colorado, about a hundred miles away from where I lived in Golden. On those Saturdays, my alarm rang around 6:30 A.M., and I returned home at 4 P.M. The entire day was shot. In the months just prior to Perry's release, I went out of a sense of duty like that of a wife in a dead marriage. My do-gooder intentions had evaporated, even though I enjoyed the repartee with Perry.

Eight months after our introduction, Perry was released to a halfway house in Denver, only thirty minutes from where I lived. I assisted him in finding a welding job, and I encouraged him to reconnect with his family. I mentally tried to prepare myself in the event Perry failed to survive back on the street. But nothing could have prepared me for the call: "I'm in trouble, man! Do you know any lawyers?"

The police had stopped him while driving with no license and no insurance. Violations while serving out a sentence in a halfway house almost always meant a quick trip back to Canon City. I was furious. His behavior had jeopardized all my neatly laid suburban plans. I had imagined him marrying his girlfriend, moving into an apartment near me, and before long, pushing his lawnmower across his front lawn and walking hand in hand with his son to the local elementary school. But instead I was walking with him up the steps to the Jefferson County Courthouse.

A lawyer was beyond Perry's finances—and mine at the time. He was stuck with me. In the pretrial meeting with the assistant district attorney, I learned that Perry had had three similar violations right before he was incarcerated three years earlier. "It doesn't look good," the attorney said. "I'll let you off on the insurance violation if you plead guilty to the driving with no license. But with your record, you'll probably have to do jail time."

"He can't do jail time," I interrupted. "He's already completing another sentence in a halfway house. There's got to be another option."

The attorney paused. "I suppose I could recommend a concurrent sentence with what he's doing now at the halfway house," she said. "That way he could remain at the halfway house and still complete his sentence. But it's still up to the judge."

Not only did the judge agree to the deal, he didn't even fine Perry. It was as if Perry hadn't committed the violation, at least as it related to his freedom.

"We did it, Dave," hollered Perry as we stepped outside the courthouse. I felt no elation. Mostly I felt disgusted with him. I brooded like the Old Testament prophet Jonah, after Nineveh repented. Perry's cockiness annoyed me. We celebrated with some ice cream, and I drove him back to the halfway house. A few months later, Perry dropped off my radar. He stopped returning my calls and, honestly, I only feigned investigating his whereabouts. Later I learned that he was back at Canon City.

I confess that I am a Shirker. I want results when I serve the poor, the imprisoned, the destitute. I want results because I want to make a difference with my life. I want purpose. Perry simply happened to be the guy who could have made that happen for me. When he didn't, I lost interest. What good is serving the poor if they don't help themselves and turn their lives around?

wow...

MY SO-CALLED SHIRKER LIFE

I'm not quite sure when I became a Shirker. It may have happened about the time my first child was born, about the time Luis threatened to kill me.

A thirty-year-old Colombian immigrant, Luis was learning English at a local church with an English as a Second Language program, and I had signed up, as I did with Perry, to befriend him and help him practice his English. I was trying to learn Spanish at the time. A couple of months after our introduction, Luis stopped attending classes. I couldn't locate him. I tracked down the number of his apartment and found out from his wife that he was on medication for a mental disorder but that he was off his meds and she believed he was going to kill her. Then Luis learned that I had called his wife. I understood enough Spanish to know that when Luis started screaming at me using the first person future tense of the Spanish verb *matar,* to kill, that I needed to find another ministry. Luis had been to our townhouse several times. I worried that my young wife might pull into our garage some afternoon to find me hanging with a Colombian necktie from the garage door braces. I abandoned my good intentions.

I quickly found another place of service with the church's contemporary worship band, where, during most services, I didn't feel as threatened.

The Shirker Life is full of service activities, mostly to and with other Shirkers. Christian service in the 'burbs is akin to volunteering as a timer or runner or finish judge at my kids' Park District swim meets. I don't actually volunteer. As a parent of a swimmer, I'm *required* to volunteer at three swim meets each season, plus the conference meet. As my wife and I mature through the cycle of young marrieds with no kids to newborns to young kids to school-aged kids, we matriculate through our church's Sunday school programs. When our kids were two, we cleaned the diapers of another Shirker's two-year-old. I'd rather walk on hot coals. And when our kids hit the teen years, we'll carpool them to the junior high lock-in.

Religion in the 'burbs tends to be more a program to join than it is an experience that changes your life. The more I participate in the programs, the further I remove myself from the deep suffering of the world. That's too bad. The entrance to the thicker, deeper life in Christ

Amen!

goes directly through the suffering of others. As soon as I discover my spiritual gifts, I am hustled into serving in one of the legion of church programs. Eventually I get to be a church leader, and I can sit for four or five hours at a setting and discuss "leveraging resources for the kingdom of God."

I often find myself serving mostly in safe or comfortable programs, where no relationship with someone in deep need forms. There doesn't appear to be any conspiracy to preclude relationships with the poor and broken. It just sort of happens, or, rather, doesn't happen. It's easier not to befriend a single mom who at forty-two with a newborn and only $6-an-hour job skills fears telling the father that he has a son because he might sue for custody because she's in such poverty. Why get involved in *that*? There's no upside. WOW...

The Shirker Life, ultimately, is a life of religious consumption—even the act of service—organized around life stages. Good Story ———↲

Take Shirker Mom, for example, who in midlife finds herself with more time for herself now that her last child has gone off to college. She wants her Shirker Husband to join her in switching churches, to one that uses words like *sacrament* and *Eucharist* instead of the *Lord's Supper*, which their current "Bible-believing" congregation uses. She has been feeling spiritually empty for some time and

DANG

feels the need for a little more mystery and symbolism in worship on Sunday mornings.

Shirker Mom can remember the first time she "accepted Jesus Christ as her personal Lord and Savior": she was six and raised her hand on the final day of vacation Bible school. A good Shirker Girl, she participated in and became a leader in the active junior high and senior high group at her Shirker Church. The teen mission trip to Tijuana, Mexico, where the team used homemade puppets to teach vacation Bible school to Mexican children, changed her life. She wanted to make a difference with her life.

A bright Shirker Teen, she decided to attend a top Christian college, where she met a Shirker Boy, and after the spring of their senior year, the Shirkers, believing that God had brought them together for a purpose, got married. Shirker Husband then landed a job in finance, and by the time the Shirkers hit thirty, they had the largest house of the five couples in their small group from church. By then the Shirker Family had expanded to two Shirker Kids. After the kids came and with Shirker Husband traveling so much, when Shirker Mom began to feel lonely for adult relationships, she joined a ministry for other Shirker Moms with preschool children. Shirker Mom loved the Bible study and spiritual friendships. She became a discussion group leader for the other Shirker Moms.

When the Shirkers' oldest, a ten-year-old, came home from school one day asking whether kissing a girl's breasts was really making out, Shirker Mom had had enough. No more public education. She was also tired of textbooks that taught only evolution, and besides, the education was better at the Shirker Christian academy, wasn't it? Didn't the kids also get an education in character? Plus, her two Shirker Boys would get solid Bible teaching and attend chapel at least three times a week. Shirker Mom was not about to leave her Shirker Kids to the sharks in the public school system. One day, as she waited for her two boys outside the Christian academy after school in her late-model black SUV, she thanked Jesus for the opportunity of a truly Christian education. She felt so blessed.

But now that both Shirker Boys were away at a Christian college, Shirker Mom felt the need for a deeper sense of Jesus in her life. For years she had heard about a charismatic mainline church in their community that, according to a neighbor who attended, also "preached the gospel." It took only one visit and she knew she had found a new spiritual home. Her spiritually passive Shirker Husband was mostly supportive; he said he never really connected with the men in their old Shirker Church anyway.

Shirker Mom loved the new angle on God and taking the Eucharist every week. (She just loved the word

Eucharist; it sounded so mysterious.) She soaked up weekly scripture readings from the Lectionary. It was as if everything she had been yearning for spiritually the past couple of years was met, finally, in this new community. Her Shirker Husband said he liked the fact that they could now sit anonymously in the pews, with no expectation to serve. He always hated being an usher. Shirker Mom missed the strong emphasis on scripture in her former Bible church, and that concerned her a bit, but she began to feel a deep sense of healing in her life. She now leads a Bible study and is excited to see other suburban moms apply scripture to their lives. It feels so good to be involved in something that makes a difference in people's lives.

The flow of Shirker Religion is all one direction: toward me (or my kids). And after my kids make it safely through high school, it's back on me again—and my need for mystery and a sense of authenticity as I move through the often muted years of midlife and beyond. Shirkers believe the Shirker thought leaders (preachers, Christian pundits, and theologians), who always frame the problems of the suburban world in terms of too little Bible and not enough truth. The solutions are always more knowledge and more teaching and more education and more content. Or it's more mystery in worship or some other new angle. Shirkers live, mostly, inside their heads.

ACTION, NOT RESULTS

My Protestant tradition has done a fabulous job of creating all sorts of assessment tools to identify my spiritual gifts. As soon as I come to faith and begin attending a church, I learn quickly that service is part of the *healthy* Christian life. I take a class on Discovering Yourself for God's Purposes and learn about my personality strengths and spiritual gifts. I feel really good about that. I don't get much of that in my work. Faith is not just about taking! It's about giving! And I get to serve in ways that I'm really good at!

Many American Christian traditions employ such assessment tools as the Meyers-Briggs Inventory, the Enneagram, DISC, and a host of other innovative, educational resources to identify people's spiritual gifts and motivate them to serve: "This is your spiritual gift. God wants you to use it to serve others. Here is a place you can serve in this church." Perhaps that is largely what makes the Christian faith unique: the emphasis on developing the human self for service to God. That may seem counterintuitive to the outside observer of Christian traditions, with all their talk of sin and the like. The parable of the three servants with differing amounts of talent in Matthew 25 has fashioned the modern American Protestant spiritual consciousness: Your talents are not really yours, but God's. Not everyone gets the same set of gifts or opportunities. Go make something happen. Your life matters. Leverage your uniqueness to make a difference.

Thus the nascent years of faith for those raised as Christians and those who come to faith in their teen years are emotionally fresh with new vistas—learning about the Bible, building new relationships, and discovering oneself in new and different ways. That plays well in the 'burbs, with its emphasis on growth and education and self-fulfillment. But the deeper life comes after that, *through* or *beyond* the discovery of self and its new vistas to a very different place.

I overheard a young suburban mother grouse recently that she had tried helping some single moms in poverty but that she had "felt used by *these* people." Then she caught herself and gave a nervous laugh: "'These people'—I guess I shouldn't say that, should I?" Apparently, she had provided some money or assistance but didn't feel appreciated. That was precisely my frustration with Perry, the convict I befriended while living in Colorado. I expected results. I expected that time plus effort equaled life change.

With so much religion and religious activities and religious resources (books, tapes, DVDs, curricula, and so on), it's difficult not to succumb to the Shirker Lifestyle.

So true . . .

Amen!

The way out of it—or actually, the way through it—is to pursue action without the thought of results or success. This is the fifth spiritual practice. You obey God's mandate to help the poor and the widows and orphans (James 1). You find a place to serve where no matter how many resources you leverage for the kingdom of God, you don't see much change. You enter into a relationship with someone of raw emotional and physical need. No doubt there are other, more sophisticated methods to make a difference in the world (protests, political influence, financial aid). But if you detach from the *emotion* and reality of the suffering of others, your soul distends. You become like Zarathustra's ghoulish image of an inverted cripple.

Too much of the Shirker Life causes bloating.

In Chapter 4, I argued that the act of facing another direction (toward those who have less than I) assists me with my hypervigilance on the possessions of others. In the act of entering into a relationship of service with no quick fixes, however, I learn about the essence of power. I absorb through experience the theological truth that only God brings about change. I don't. I don't leverage anything. I'm not saying that serving in the junior high ministry is not worthy. It is. But it's not what most 'burb types need to walk farther into the kingdom of Jesus.

Most likely, if I'm serving in the junior high ministry, it's because of my kids, an extension of my ego: "The most important thing we can do is make sure our kids know Jesus and find good friends. You don't know how tough it is out there in the secular world."

Who can argue with that? I'm not. I'm simply saying that when you feel the thirst for more of Jesus, find a hopeless case or a hopeless cause.

I once heard a woman in late midlife say that "after you give them a little money to pay their rent and buy some food, all you can do, really, is pray with them." She was referring to the homeless at the local shelter. I wanted to argue with her. But she has given a large portion of the second half of her life to teaching English to the refugees filling our suburb and to coordinating the food pantry ministry of a local church. Hers isn't the stereotyped fundamentalism, which would rather save your soul from hell than feed you for a day. Her wisdom is aged in the reality of a lifetime of action. The thicker life is characterized by action (the cup of cold water in Jesus' name) but without the need for the fruits of action (self-fulfillment or success).

After I do all I can to help Perry make it on the street, I pray for him. It's all, really, that is left to do. And finally, Perry isn't the hopeless case. I am. I need to help Perry as much or more than he needs help from me.

[margin note: We use prayer as a last resort, and view it as giving up + doing nothing.]

BEYOND OUTCOMES

One suburban family, with five kids between three and sixteen, has for the past ten years helped refugees from places like Africa establish a new life in our western Chicago suburbs. The results are mixed—for both the refugees *and* the Johnson family. Kevin is a software developer, and Judy, a former nurse, is a stay-at-home mom. The high point was the Armenian family from Azerbaijan who, within five years after Kevin met them at Chicago O'Hare Airport, bought their first suburban home. Their two kids even made it to college. The low point was the Cuban who committed a felony and ended up paying for it in a downstate correctional facility.

The refugees deboard at Chicago's Midway or O'Hare Airport alone, always, with little or no personal belongings. Kevin and Judy volunteer as sponsors with a local relief organization that helps the refugees find housing and English classes and other basic social services. Volunteers assemble a welcome package that includes only the very practical: sheets, pillows, blankets, food staples. They meet them at the airport, and the relationship begins.

"They have nothing when they arrive," said Kevin, "but what they really need is a friend." And a buffer from American marketing.

"We win car!" One afternoon, Kevin fielded an excited call from the mom of a refugee family and hustled over to their apartment to find out what had been won. A fast food chain had come out with a marketing campaign that promised a Dodge Viper to anyone who scratched off a winning combination of codes on fountain drink cups. When Kevin arrived at the apartment, plastic cups were everywhere.

The kids had gotten two of the three needed stickers to win the car. Believing the third was just a few Cokes away, the refugees kept purchasing fountain drinks. With the family's limited English, Kevin's message wasn't easy to communicate: It's the third cup with the winning number that you never get. Kevin read to them the promotion's fine-print rules. The odds of winning were one in ten million. He finally convinced them that the game was simply a ruse to get them to buy the drinks. One of the family members mused, "What does that say about us?" Kevin didn't have a reply.

"You must have a relationship with them," says Kevin, "or they won't tell you what they need. But anyone who can function in America can help a refugee."

I asked Kevin and Judy about their kids; certainly their work with refugees has shaped how their kids view the world. They paused and looked at each other. "It was easier when our kids were younger," Judy said. "They played together with the kids of the refugees when our families got together. But now that our oldest are in their teens, they have little in common with the teens of the refugee families."

The Johnsons went so far as to purchase a home with mother-in-law quarters, handy when a refugee needs short-term housing. They say they are compelled by the Old Testament notion of how people of faith should honor strangers in their midst. Yet, even for those bitten by the call to serve refugees, it's never convenient. "Almost every time in the past ten years that we needed to visit one of our refugee families," said Kevin, "especially those who were located about forty minutes away, I thought, *Oh no, we have to see the refugees this week.* We had to make ourselves go."

That is the hard part of obedience, when you do it out of sheer commitment. It's especially difficult when there seem to be no real results or sense of significance. It's old-fashioned obedience to what God has asked you to do.

A friend who volunteers at the local homeless shelter says it has not been a radically transforming spiritual experience. For a few years, he carped about how the inter-church homeless ministry relegates evangelism to the periphery, how it has aggravated homelessness by treating the homeless as guests, and so on. But in the course of working breakfast, dinner, and midnight shifts, he has learned to let go of his preconceptions of the "successful homeless ministry" and begin to simply learn to *be with* the homeless. His most rewarding moments come after breakfast is served when he stands with the smokers outdoors in the patio, talking with them, mostly just listening to their stories—often narcissistic and far-fetched tales of injustices visited upon them, but sometimes poignant narratives of lives gone terribly awry.

"I'm still not very good at entering into their suffering," he says, "but my life is so sheltered with material blessings and psychologically healthy friends, it's better than nothing. At least once a month, I'm forced to think about those who genuinely suffer."

As I progress spiritually, I should feel less need to do only that which promotes my self and the extension of my self (my kids, for example). My life becomes a reverse flow. Instead of collecting religious experiences, I expend myself with no thought of results.

Michael Molinos, the sixteenth-century Christian mystic, wrote, "We labor without personal interest. We labor merely for the glory of God. . . . We are like the young men who work in the field with their father. At the end of the day, unlike the hired labor, we receive no pay.

Great!

"But at the end of the year, we enjoy all things."[5]

What we enjoy, after being released from the need for significance and success, is the sweetness of the obedience. Finding one's purpose comes not from the results of service but from the act of obedience. No matter what the call—resettling refugees, championing affordable housing for the poor or cheap drugs to combat AIDS, fighting for human rights, or the simple act of buying a cup of coffee for an older woman who sits alone on the bench outside Starbucks—inner liberty comes as I pursue truth, justice, and righteousness without needing to be seen as right or needing to see results. The odyssey into the thicker life in God is always "active and practical, not passive and theoretical. It is an organic life-process . . . which the whole self does; not something as to which its intellect holds an opinion."[6]

Of course, to use a cliché, that's more of a journey than it is a destination.

7

Lashed Down

Environmental Toxin: "My church is the problem."
Spiritual Practice: Staying put in your church

In 1992, my wife, Jana, and I, newly married, moved from the Front Range area of Colorado to the western Chicago suburbs. A few months afterward, Jana and I drove north in a cold spring rain to Door County, Wisconsin, a beautiful, timbered resort area, for a Memorial Weekend jaunt. We hoped the weekend would warm up, but its romance cooled Sunday when I made a flippant remark about the church Jana grew up in.

Our recent move to Illinois had put us in Jana's hometown, and we were in the process of deciding whether to attend her home church, the one her father, who had passed away suddenly in 1973, had helped start almost fifty years earlier. The covert pressure I felt from Jana and her family irked me. I knew how such comments irked my wife. I was only newly married, but I should have been smarter than that.

We patched things up after the lost weekend and settled on Jana's home church, which we attend to this day. During our first few years there, I carped that "this church is poorly organized"; "it's friendly only to the insiders"; and "it's too bound by tradition." If not for the fact that my wife's mother and brother attended the church, I might have insisted we find another. Actually, I may still be in denial in thinking that attending elsewhere was ever an option. It wasn't that I didn't like the people in the church; I had made friends quickly. But perhaps at least some of my resistance was genetic.

Around age forty, my grandfather underwent a conversion experience on the prairies of South Dakota. Although reared in a God-fearing family, he had never experienced the enthusiasm and energy and joy that his newfound faith would generate. As the story has been passed down to me, Grandpa's conversion to a more firebrand and pious Christianity was the result of Pentecostal winds that swept over the prairies in the early 1950s. Overnight Grandpa went from passive God-fearer to inspired man of God.

That, apparently, posed a threat to the pastor at the little church in a prairie village a few miles east of my grandfather's farm. Details are sketchy (and I gathered them only from family sources), but a conflict arose between my grandfather and the pastor. My grandfather felt the pastor was "liberal" and didn't believe in the "new birth." That the pastor allegedly smoked and drank didn't help much. Apparently the pastor had attended a seminary in Yankton, South Dakota, considered by some to be theologically liberal. Even in the prairie villages of the Dakotas in the middle of the twentieth century, the modernist-fundamentalist controversy raged.

In a church business meeting, the animosity between the two flared. The pastor asked my grandfather, who was the church secretary recording minutes of the business meeting, to come to the front of the church. According to my father, when my grandfather got to the front, the pastor ripped the record book out of his hands and shouted, "Get out!" When my grandfather and his family walked out of the church that day, several of my grandfather's siblings and their families followed. The church closed its doors not long after.

Never again would my grandfather join a church as an official member, though throughout his life he regularly attended various churches in the outlying communities. He was always at church on Sunday, even teaching Sunday school sometimes. But he often participated in Bible studies at one church while attending worship at another. I recall my grandfather saying, "God is going to bring all denominations together some day." Until his sudden death in 1987, Grandpa, whom I admired deeply, was an advocate of the universal body of Christ—that is, all believers in Christ are united as one in Christ. He had little tolerance for denominations and church loyalty.

So I come by my resistance to staying put in one church honestly. I knew that once Jana and I began attending "her" church, her long history there would lash us to it. My freedom to circulate in the extended body of Christ would be restricted. With no or little experience of strong church ties, I simply didn't know what a commitment to a local body of believers over a long period of time really meant.

Freedom does not always mean going. In the thicker life, in fact, freedom often means staying. That's certainly true of the Christian understanding of marriage. Staying with one partner over a lifetime opens me up to the goodness of God in a way that serial monogamy doesn't. Church is another place where freedom means staying. That seems counterintuitive, given scripture's emphasis on the kingdom of God and its global enterprise. With both church and marriage, in a culture of options, I choose not to move. I stay rooted in community, because only in a place where I'm free not to leave can I find the "personal" in the so-called personal relationship with God. This sixth practice is all about staying in relationships when everything inside me screams to pack up my hurt feelings and find a more ideal community.

CASUAL SEX LOYALTY

For almost fifteen years, I've stayed put in one church, thanks to the family ties that bind (and certainly *not* because of my deep spirituality), while observing the migration patterns of my highly mobile religious community.

[Suburban church consumerism has been lamented for years. And I can't say that rural church loyalty is any deeper. Rural churches suffer from the consumer disease as well. Deeper family ties may obviate, though, some of the extreme forms of church mobility seen in the suburbs. My point in this book is not that the hazards of suburbia can't be found elsewhere. They just seem to be intensified in my mostly white-collar community.]

While I haven't conducted a national study, my community may boast the nation's most mobile churchgoing members. There are simply so many good options, depending on your life stage and worship preference.

For decades, denominational loyalty has been thinning. Much research has been conducted on the realities of the postdenominational world. Many are the reasons why Catholics become Protestants, Protestants become Catholics, Protestants become Orthodox, Low Protestants become High Protestants, and so forth. The flow seems to go in all directions, though not, obviously, at the same rate.

Religious experts have observed that the invention of

the automobile and modern communications may have reshaped the American religious landscape more than anything else. Television revealed to us that our pastor is really not that engaging when compared to the NBC anchor of the evening news or even the television preacher. The car provided the means to attend the church in the next 'burb with the better communicator or great kids' programs. Religious folks may drive by fifteen churches to get to the one they want. In many communities, the neighborhood church has been overshadowed by large regional churches. People *commute* to church. If it takes twenty-seven minutes to get to the good preaching and great programs, it's worth it, just as it is to cart your daughter to the better violin teacher two suburbs over.

Within my Protestant family, many churchgoing folk change churches as if they were changing drycleaners. If they come across a coupon for a dime less per laundered shirt, they're off to another store. Actually, I think it may be less like shopping and more like casual sex.

It's certainly not about ongoing relationships. It's about the immediate experience, the brief sensation of feeling like I have finally found a home, a place where I deeply resonate with the worship and theology (at least for a time).

It's one year here and two years there, back to the first church to patch things up, and then on to the cool church with the *authentic* charismatic liturgy where you can find inner healing. Few, except for frustrated clergy, admit that local church loyalty is this thin; the reasons offered by church migrants (when someone bothers to ask) always seem reasonable. Often the reason goes back to the kids: "There's no youth program for our kids, and we know that over at First Church, they have a large youth program. And we really want our kids to make good friends."

Parents will lay down their lives if their kids' spirituality and social needs appear to be at stake. It would be better to slap the cub of a she-grizzly than to suggest to any suburban parent that perhaps there are considerations other than the immediate welfare of kids for making decisions. I've often been taken aback at how bitter parents of teenagers seem when the topic of the youth pastor comes up: "He doesn't call my son. Leaving a message on voicemail isn't good enough. My son doesn't fit in."

wow
so
true

So clergy take the hit. One person candidly told me that one reason he and his family evacuated one suburb and shuttled their possessions to another farther west was that they "weren't getting fed" by their pastor. By buying a house in a suburb thirty minutes away, they could more tastefully explain to their church friends why they were leaving: "We needed a church closer to our new home." "Not getting fed" and "not biblical enough" are common complaints about preaching. I personally would add "anything over twenty-four minutes."] *Ha!*

Church migration patterns tend to follow whatever church has the buzz—the "more biblical" preacher; the newer, more authentic service with the riveting young pastor who weaves stories using live animals as props and uses technology innovatively; the *nuevo* liturgical service; the burgeoning youth ministry with the exotic mission trips. There's nothing like momentum, when your church is the one that is attracting new attendees. There's nothing worse than seeing your friends leave your church for another only a mile or so away.

The religious hoi polloi seem restless, always looking for the next worship conquest. Often the anxiety is couched in terms of life change: "Our oldest is now a senior, and she'll be headed to college in the fall. We just need a place that ministers to me and my husband for a change." "We're really tired of worship choruses and casual Protestantism. We want a church that is steeped in mystery and transcendence." "We need a church that is a healing place." "After the tough years in dealing with our son, we just need a place where no one knows us for that. We want to be anonymous, where we can sit in the pew and just be ourselves." And of course, there are always the theological reasons: "The church is headed in a direction that is not biblical."

One Sunday a couple visiting our church for the first time asked to interview me and several others, including my wife Jana, during the Sunday school hour following the first service. The couple said they had decided to leave their church because of a disagreement with the senior pastor and that they wanted to make sure that their new church had a well thought-out plan for handling conflict. At the time, I was part of the church leadership.

During the interview, it became clear the couple was looking for a specific answer. I wasn't much help. I fumbled a bit, trying to say that yes, we try to handle conflict among members in a Christ-honoring way. The couple wasn't impressed. I found myself trying to anticipate what they wanted to hear. [Toward the end, one of our team said to the woman, "What gifts do you bring to a church? How do you think you could serve here?" "I'd rather not talk about that," she replied. The interview was over, and we never saw them again. Choice is a beautiful thing.]

True...

While I'm sympathetic to the challenges of suburban church ministry and the competitive realities created by the automobile and modern communications, Protestant clergy must accept at least some of the responsibility. A colleague attends a church whose messy staff conflict sent attendees scurrying to find new houses of worship. By the conflict's end, many of his friends, fed up with

the senior pastor's doubletalk, began attending elsewhere. All the members of his small group eventually left
the church (though none left the small group, which still
meets regularly in homes). In our community, I have observed clergy shamelessly recruiting leaders from area
churches. One convinced a committed family in another
church to serve in his by saying he had a "word of
prophecy" from the Lord. Clergy say they hate the mobility, but when you score a new couple with three kids
under twelve, for some the philosophy may be "Don't
ask, don't tell."

Some churches plain and simple don't deserve a lick
of loyalty. Some of my churchgoing friends carp that
their church's lay leaders would rather discuss reaching
out than truly "welcome the stranger," as set forth by the
Old Testament; that the preaching is mostly anemic; that
the pastor is either an autocrat or a people pleaser; or that
worship has the energy of a Sunday afternoon after an ex-
hausting dinner.

I truly am amazed that any American attends church.
I'm not particularly disheartened by national studies that
indicate dwindling attendance. In a society with few constraints for church attendance, that a quarter of the population, at least in the Midwest, attends church with
some regularity should delight the religious pundits. Of
course, they see the pews as only half empty.

I myself can't help but be tempted by the grand American vision of the spiritual life: sitting alone on a bluff overlooking a glassy mountain lake, contemplating the silence and the aspen leaves that are turning to gold and red while pulling up my Patagonia fleece around my neck and anticipating the $4 coffee that my wife is picking up from the corporate coffee shop just up the road. Grandpa and Grandma have the kids, of course.

Now *that* is what I call *real* church: me and Jesus. It feels so authentic. No messy relationships. No commitment. No social constraints to serve in the two-year-old room and change the diapers of someone else's kid. Go Jesus. *So true...*

CHURCH AS CANNIBALISM

DANG

If I had been a marketing consultant to the apostle Paul and his cronies, I probably would have encouraged them to find a model other than the local Jewish synagogues: "If you really want brand extension, think bigger. Local worshipping communities of families are fine as far as they go. But I'd emphasize the 'universal body of Christ' thing. That is scalable. That's global. And by the way, ditch the whole 'carry your cross' thing. You really can't leverage that. It's too hard to explain in PowerPoint."

While completing seminary, I worked as a youth director in a small Protestant congregation that, as part of its liturgy, offered Communion only one Sunday a month. One Sunday, the young wife of a brain surgeon said to me, "I'm not coming to church anymore on the first Sunday of the month, but I'll still drop off the kids." She was new to our church—and new to church, period. "I really don't get the 'eat the flesh' and 'drink the blood' part of Communion. That sounds creepy to me, like cannibalism."

Church is strange. It's simply different from any other kind of organization or experience in the industrialized world. No matter how my Protestant tradition tries to stay culturally relevant (and I'm the first to embrace innovation), sacraments such as Communion, Baptism, and, of course, the Passing of the Offering Plate, are just plain bizarre. Even if the worship band is playing speed metal.

LOL

In *The Four Loves,* C.S. Lewis points out that nature, for all its staggering beauty, is limited for the seeker of God; natural beauty can't communicate God's truths about salvation and the contemplative life. To move in a Godward direction, nature seekers are better served by the local church:

> Nature cannot satisfy the desires she arouses nor answer theological questions nor sanctify us. Our

real journey to God involves constantly turning our backs on her; passing from the dawn-lit fields into some pokey little church, or (it might be) going to work in an East End Parish.[1]

For all its foibles—lousy preaching, political infighting, self-centered focus, stagnation—the pokey local church in suburbia is still one of the most fertile environments for spiritual development. All churches, for that matter, are pokey, even the large, corporate churches, because they are led by pokey leaders and attended by pokey members. Pokiness always breeds trouble. And relational trouble is the stuff of the deeper life. As much as I feel closer to Jesus while I'm fly-fishing a small high mountain lake in the Collegiate Wilderness in the Rockies, the experience doesn't do much for moving me Godward. The experience just creates a warm memory. It's spiritually jejune.

Without a long-term attachment to a pokey local church, there is little spiritual deepening—even if your new church takes you into the "mysteries of God" in a way your old church couldn't.

I'm all for improving the local church to make it more effective at its biblical mandates. The maddening frustration that prompts someone to leave one church for another, however, may be precisely the experience that *WOW...* triggers spiritual progress if one stays. German pastor and martyr Dietrich Bonhoeffer captured the essence of this truth: *READ*

> Just as surely as God desires to lead us to a knowledge of genuine Christian fellowship, so surely must we be overwhelmed by a great disillusionment with others, with Christians in general, and, if we are fortunate, with ourselves.... Only that fellowship which faces such disillusionment, with all its unhappy and ugly aspects, begins to be what it should be in God's sight, begins to grasp in faith the promise that is given to it.[2]

Without hitching myself to a local body of believers, my spiritual development mutates. The eye of the soul begins to close. While it is true that those of faith exist as part of the universal spiritual body of Christ—an elementary Christian doctrine that in my grandfather's later years supported his wandering church habits—the church on the corner of First and Main is where the action is. The real journey to God involves, at least in part, the *relationships* of the worshipping community. I can pick up dozens of books on worship styles or emerging worship trends or what a religious curmudgeon believes constitutes authentic worship, but nothing about the practical theology of the relationships of worship.

It's too bad that only the religious hegemony write on these topics.

Too much of the current discussion of worship practices and trends creates an idol out of corporate worship. What if corporate worship doesn't matter? At least not like we think it does. I said that once while enjoying Chicago-style stuffed pizza with a friend who thinks deeply about the theology of worship, and he about throttled me. The final piece didn't taste as good.

What if the *relationships* of the worshipping community matter more than we think?

What if church mobility, and our proclivity to slough off relationships, tells us something about our understanding of the Trinity, an elemental tenet of those who consider themselves orthodox?

What if a God of Relationships does give a hoot about the *relationships* of the worshipping community? What if part of worshipping God in spirit and truth is honoring the relationships that the gathered community automatically creates?

What if church loyalty should be less like casual sex and more like monogamy?

Boring, I know, but what if? *DANG*

Should my church relationships be as transient as those with the Park District families who show up at my kids' soccer practices and games? I see them for a couple of months in the fall and again in the spring, but that's about it, except for Starbucks now and then.

A Montana acquaintance and I once discussed the differences between church in the 'burbs and church in rural areas. I grew up in rural communities and now live in the suburbs. He was raised in the suburbs and at the time pastored a church in a rural community. He said that in a rural environment, church is just one of many contexts in which a person interacts with the community. For example, my grandfather, when he was booted out of the church, still sat next to former church members at the sale barn, where cattle get auctioned off, or at community gatherings, such as at the volunteer fire department's annual pancake breakfast. No doubt my grandfather's hasty exit strained some relationships, but his leaving didn't necessarily cut him off from them.

That's not true in my suburban community. If I left my church for another, most likely my church relationships would drift off. Few are the community functions at which I interact meaningfully with people from my church—only an occasional soccer game or back-to-school night.

JOE AND JANE SHALLOW

Meet the Perpetual Spiritual Adolescent (PSA). She may be as biblically and philosophically educated as a professor of Christian theology, sated with knowledge. He may be the classic passive sports and finance guy. Both are stuck. You'd think that the Bible-minded person would have an inside track to the Godhead. But more Bible or theological knowledge doesn't seem to translate into spiritual maturity. To the "O Knowledgeable One," church never meets her expectations. It's never deep enough or right enough. Knowledge tends mostly to breed cynicism and self-righteousness, not spirituality. The apostle Paul said that knowledge puffs up. It does. And to the passive sports and finance guy, the laconic pew warmer, church is boring as hell.

AMEN!

WOW!

Both types are perpetually disillusioned with the church. Both are prone to pay fealty to a charismatic church leader. And when the pastor or priest moves on, they move on. Both keep church relationships largely at an emotional distance. Nobody or nothing is good enough, or everybody's a hypocrite.

There is no clear PSA profile, of course, other than the person who always externalizes the problems at church. People are too rich, too white, too shallow, too old, too ingrown, too radical, too boring, too hypocritical, too stiff, too Pentecostal, too conservative, too liberal, too whatever. It's church, for Pete's sake! It's supposed to be broken. Jesus must see something in the church that I don't.

wow... good!

The disillusionment with my church is real, and every person who has spent much time in church has experienced it. But it's the getting stuck part that predestines me to a Peter Pan spirituality. What if disillusionment with church, though, is a precursor to the promises of God, as Bonhoeffer suggests?

The doorway to the thicker life opens with a profound weariness with church. To walk through it, though, means to move from "He is the problem" to "I am part of the problem." Something happens in that transition. It is always easier to leave than to go deep. But to go deep is to stay, and that's the life practice: staying put long enough in a community of worshippers for your feelings to get hurt. Or for you to disagree with the direction of the church. When everything inside you screams to leave, you stay. You stay to see what God will create in your life and in the pokey local church.

What I perceive to be *my* needs—"I need a church with a preacher who uses specific examples from real life"—may not correspond to my true spiritual needs. Often, in fact, I am not attuned to my true spiritual needs. Staying put is a spiritual discipline that allows

God's grace to work on unsanded surfaces of my inner life. The biggest problem in any church I attend is my love of self.

I once overheard someone observe, acerbically, that his aging mother had attended church for forty years while never appearing to grow spiritually. While that may be possible, though it's a long shot to judge accurately someone's spirituality, more likely spiritual progress will be disabled by serial monogamy. Staying put and immersing oneself in the life of a worshipping body forces one into eventual conflict with other church members or with the church leadership or both. Frustration and conflict are the fabric of spiritual development.

Many of the popular reasons given for a new church conquest are actually spiritual reasons for staying put. They are a means of grace, preventing talk of spirituality from becoming sentimental or philosophical. Biblical spirituality is always earthy, face to face, and often messy. Never abstract. And often not all that mystical.

OLD NATURE CURE

Only in relationships that permit no bailing out can certain forms of spiritual development occur. Marriage is one. Church is another.

In a recent congregational meeting, two young male professionals made a presentation to update the sanctuary sound system. Their pitch was well delivered. As they began fielding questions, an older gentleman challenged the presenter's use of a technical term. I don't remember the exact phrasing that sparked the fireworks, but the atmosphere in our fellowship hall, which was a little tense because the sound system upgrade involved a significant amount of money, suddenly intensified. The young presenter and this retired attorney began to quarrel about who was right, as if they were the only two in the room. I began to feel embarrassed for the older gentleman, since his comment and persistence had provoked and sustained the interchange. There's nothing more uncomfortable in a church meeting than an older man needing to be right. *woah...*

The discussion ended awkwardly with the congregation voting to upgrade the sound system, and the meeting came to a close. Afterward, I saw the elderly gentleman amble toward where the presenter sat. Later I heard from others who overheard that conversation: the elderly gentlemen asked the young professional out for breakfast to discuss the project.

I don't know if the breakfast ever happened or whether the two reconciled. But that's the stuff of church and the stuff of spirituality. At its best, the local church functions as an arena in which conflict and hurts among participants who choose to stay can open up possibilities for spiritual progress. Where else will people still accept me after I stand up in a church meeting and harshly criticize something? "Ah, that's just Dave," they say. They know me. I learn about the Christian virtues of acceptance and graciousness even when I am not accepting and gracious. By not taking my toys and playing elsewhere—finding a church that agrees with me—I move forward in my spiritual journey.

Ha!

Besides a mother-in-law, there is no social suburban constraint for the discipline of staying put in your current church. I can't be too self-righteous about my church tenure, after all. I am grateful for it. Our church recently went through a period of decline—an awkward pastoral change and then giving down, attendance down, momentum down. I was undone when several core families left the church for one on a growth curve across our suburb. I stewed, ranted to my wife, and then realized that I was mostly sad. I missed those folks. And in many ways, I can't blame them for leaving. I'd probably change churches every couple of years if it weren't for our family roots. I don't have much in the way of character for stay-

Ha!

ing. Not only am I a Protestant (with the "protest and leave" DNA), I am, after all, an entrepreneur. I like all things new. And entrepreneurs, even in the boring Midwest, would always rather move than stay. I hope I'm not too flippant about my religious tradition's penchant to split and start anew. I am at peace with it.

Even in decent marriages, monogamy vacillates between lows and highs, with lots of monotony in between. It's during the lowest of the lows that staying as a spiritual discipline goes to work on my overblown sense of self, and my naïve, conscious judgment of what I think I need spiritually. Seventeenth-century French Catholic mystic François Fénelon wrote, "Slowly you will learn that all the troubles in your life—your job, your health, your inward failings—are really cures to the poison of your old nature."[3]

I would add "your church" to his list. Thank God for disillusionment.

8

Spiritual Friendship

Environmental Toxin: "What will this relationship do for me?"
Spiritual Practice: Building deep and meaningful friendships

N othing good can come of this."

My wife's throwaway comment turned out to be prescient. Our oldest had just discovered eBay and was whining like only an eight-year-old can to buy a trading card. It was Slifer the Sky Dragon. It was $27.

"But it's *my* money."

"You're right," I said. "It's your money." *This could be a good lesson.* I reached for a credit card, and he handed me a portion of his savings.

As soon as the card arrived, Christian traded it. In return he received a handful of "minor league" cards. A day later, as Jana urged the kids into our minivan after school, she said, "Your dad won't be happy that you traded the card." (I hadn't really grasped yet the concept that trading cards are for, well, trading.) The classic first child, Christian panicked. He ran back out onto the schoolyard and demanded that his friend trade back to their original positions. His friend said it was fine but that he would have to go home to get the card.

The next afternoon, home early from work, I asked Christian if his friend had returned the card. He had. I glanced at the card and noticed that the foil around the edges of Slifer had been marked with a pencil.

"What happened to your card?" I said. "Did you do that?"

"No."

"Well, then, your friend must have done it. The card was new two days ago. I think you should go over to your friend's house and ask him why he ruined your card."

"I'll just call him."

"I think you should talk to him face to face."

"I want to call him."

Christian called while I was seated in the dining room. I overheard him try to explain to his friend that the card was ruined. He said he wondered why his friend had scribbled on the card.

"He says he didn't do it," Christian whispered to me.

"Well, who else did it?"

"You talk to him."

"I don't want to talk to him."

Christian thrust the phone into my hands. Suddenly, I was ear to ear with his friend. I can't remember what I said. It was along the lines of "Christian feels bad because the card that he traded to you is ruined."

His friend denied the deed, and I handed the phone back to Christian. Later that evening, around 8:00, the phone rang. I didn't pick up. We had an answering machine (and not voice mail). I heard the caller: "This is _____'s dad. He told me about a little incident with a trading card. Could you call me later tonight?" The tone of his voice made me feel uneasy, my adrenaline stirring. I'd act like a grownup: *I'll let the boys deal with this.*

When I returned the call a half hour later, I tried to make light banter as the conversation began. I didn't know the man and certainly didn't want to convey that I was at all emotionally implicated.

"After _____ hung up, he cried," the boy's father said. "He was scared of you. He said you yelled at him. If you want to talk to my boy, you need to go through me. What kind of man are you to yell at an eight-year-old boy?"

I shuddered with anger. I said as coolly as I could, "Well, I think perhaps we disagree on how I talked to your son. I wouldn't describe what I said to him as yelling. I'm sorry he perceived our conversation that way."

I said the card had been defaced. He rationally pointed out that the deal was between the two boys, implying who the hell was I to force his son to trade back the card. The conversation spiraled downward for a few minutes until at last the father said, "A deal's a deal. Whatever my son did to the card when it was in his possession is legally his right to do."

He had me.

"You're absolutely right," I said. "Legally, your son could do whatever he wanted." I barely held back from saying what was next on my mind: *But friends don't do that to each other.*

Like nice suburban folk, we politely said our goodbyes, and the matter was put, awkwardly, to rest. It certainly didn't seem to nick the boys' friendship. I too would have been a little ripped if my son had been accused by an adult of something he denied. Your son is always right.

Boys learn early, though, that many relationships are more or less like a deal. You get what you get in the deal. Later, after you complete your law degree or MBA, you learn it's good business when the deal is win-win, instead of win-lose. What transpired in the card trade was great training for the so-called real world. Transactional relationships get you the good jobs, the next deal, the inside track to senior management. No one ever made it to the top ranks on performance and hard work alone. You give to get. When you get, you give back.

Spiritual friendship is subversive in an environment of transaction and efficiency. The seventh life practice is finding and deepening the relationships that provide me the kind of community that meets some of my deepest longings. Friendship subverts the system of power, how things get done in the 'burbs and the class system organized around symbols of immortality.

ECONOMICS OF RELATIONSHIPS

I work in the so-called real world. I engineered the client list of my marketing company through transactional relationships. I was a slow study the first few years of my business, with low emotional intelligence; I couldn't figure out the most basic function of a business: landing the next client. It was a classic case of "I can help you do it, but I can't do it for myself."

I seem to learn only through financial pain, so I picked up the art of business by referral: I help you so you can help me (and refer new clients to me). I subscribed to motivational speaker Zig Ziglar's philosophy that if you help people with what they want, you can have everything you want. I ask about your kids, your Jackson Hole vacation—as if I really care—so that I can meet some of your needs. And then, knowing that every person is only six degrees from every other person, I ask you to do something for me: Would you refer me to your friend, the chief marketing officer over at XYZ Corporation? I think our firm could really help them build deeper client loyalty.

Writer F. Scott Fitzgerald once noted that Ernest Hemingway "would always give a helping hand to a man on a ledge a little higher up."[1] That is the essence of the transactional relationship.

I make friends easily, and I've had to use that to my advantage in business because no one turns a head when I walk into a room. No one has ever said I fill a room with my presence. By the evening's end, though, many in the room have told me something they regret saying later. When I worked for one organization, one of the vice presidents complained that he had to come to me, a mid-level manager, to find out what actually transpired at the vice presidents meeting (which he had attended but I hadn't). My business began to grow when I franchised my ability to ask questions and then listen while people ran on about themselves. Next thing I knew, people called me friend, and the business started to take off.

I struggle, though, to imagine a relationship sustained by something other than utility. Take, even, our friendships with some of our kids' elementary school teachers. I wonder if my wife and I would be as chummy with them if they hadn't fawned over our kids and described them as "exceptional." They tell us our kids are bright, and we praise their teaching acumen. We hang with them at the PTA-sponsored fifties dance and accept their invitations to parties outside school. It feels so righteous to be part of the in-crowd at the local elementary school.

Truth be told, many suburban relationships tend to be positioned by my accumulation of immortality symbols: my above-average kids, the SUV, the two-week vacations, and where my home sits in relation to the more expensive neighborhoods in Wheaton. I was dumbfounded when our twelve-year-old babysitter noticed that we had traded up to an SUV. "I really like your truck, Mr. Goetz." She didn't say it only once. And when a bass guitar-playing thirteen-year-old with dark curly locks, the son one of my brother-in-law's friends, went out of his way to say he admired my "ride," I actually felt a little smug, followed by the thought that I was such a loser.

In the 'burbs, athletic kids, perhaps the crowning immortality symbol, often facilitate adult friendships. Parents form season-long relationships while commuting to games and shuffling kids to practices. The friendships may be thin, though, arising largely around the perceived collaboration of team goals. The friendships stick as long as the stress of competition stays in check. Parents overinvested in victory may begin to carp, though, about some-one else's child who seems to be underproducing. I've had fathers complain to me when my elementary-age son struck out in Park District baseball. Often the child of the parent criticizing the other teammates hears the re-marks. They can unstitch the team.

An Episcopalian priest who has raised two kids in a high-rent community says, "Friendship, when the adults have children, is often undermined by competition and recognition of youth achievements. Such friendships work as long as victory continues." Winning itself is the transactional glue.

Recently our outwardly economically egalitarian neighborhood with small ranch-style homes built in the 1950s has been invaded by what are called "tear-downs." Builders tear down a $350,000 home to erect a $1 mil-lion one. Small-time builders walk our neighborhoods like Mormon missionaries, preaching the gospel of selling your home for "cash, with no realtor expenses." Everyone has his price, we're told. The home next to ours went down this summer, and our quiet street was abuzz with gossipy speculation about who our neighbors might be. Would they like us, living in squalor next to them? One assumption in our conversations: that we'd likely have with the new ostensibly monied neighbors a different kind of relationship than we had with each other.

Is our neighborliness based on immortality symbols—only those within the same price range?

When my wife and I moved to the Midwest, we moved into my wife's 'hood. While I can make conversation with a toad, the intricate Midwestern social lattice put my skills to the test. I noticed that the questions after a weekend, for example, were different. In Colorado, people asked, "Where did you go this weekend?" In Illinois, they asked, "What did you *do* this weekend?" People here really don't go places on weekends. You mow the lawn, visit Home Depot, paint a bathroom. Yes, some fight the traffic to Wisconsin or Michigan, but not every weekend. In Colorado, you're always heading to the mountains, even after the Thanksgiving meal. In Illinois, we head to the living room afterward to sit and recall old stories and look at each other for several hours. It took about eight Thanksgiving and Christmas seasons before someone finally, after the big meal, turned to me and said, "Now Dave, what do you do for a living?" I was an outsider, albeit an in-law. I had to earn the right through tenure to enter the social conversation.

For those on the outside, the social rules for community feel transactional.

Several years back, I assisted our church in its small group ministry. One goal was to help newer people build deeper relationships with others in the church. We recruited the new folks to meet in homes with eight to twelve people every other week. I noticed that when we allowed groups to form by choice, they often did so around economic stations. My wife and I participated in a small group that met every other week for almost ten years with summers off. We all had young kids. We all lived in what would be considered starter homes or perhaps one level up. Everyone owned a home, and no one lived in what 'burbanites call a starter castle (the really big homes). Even (or especially) in church, relationships tend to form around economics. From what I've observed, upper-middle-class church folks rarely cross the threshold of the homes of lower-income folks in the church. And middle-class folks with homes never hold their small group meeting in one of the apartments. If you are lucky **WOW...** enough to be in a small group with members in a higher income bracket than yours, you don't raise your hand when asked to host the next small group meeting. You stick with bringing the brownies.

While I served as a youth director at a small church in what would now be called the exurbs of Denver, I was asked to report at a building-committee meeting on future spacing needs for the youth. While the committee members gathered, I overheard an older businessman, tall and barrel-chested, ask a newcomer to the committee, "And what do *you* do for a living?" The question had an edge to it, almost a sneer. I took the man to imply that the newcomer, who was his junior by twenty years, six inches, and a hundred pounds, had no business being on the committee. The fresh recruit replied, "I'm a pediatric ophthalmologist. I have my own practice." The businessman paused and blinked several times, and then welcomed him heartily to the group. Even in church, what you do (a man's ultimate immortality symbol)—and thus who you are—matters. You are welcomed into my coterie if you measure up. Many church relationships are, in essence, transactional: "Your economic status builds me up, and makes me feel good about me. I will have a relationship with you. I will invite you into my starter-castle circle."

My neighbor, a young pastor of a growing suburban congregation, says that intimacy is the one thing in his church that everyone craves but few seem to have. You can't use relationships as a means to position yourself in life and then also expect to experience in them the kind of friendship that sweetens life and takes the edge off its hard parts.

Obviously, most, if not all, relationships have transactional traces in them. I gain from friendship, I give in friendship. Yet true friendship is one of the great gifts of the thicker life and subverts the politics of community in suburbia.

FULLY KNOWN

There are not many classic spirituality works on friendship, and perhaps for good reason.

If you write abstractly on the topic, it becomes reading for insomniacs. If you write a first-person account of a friendship, at least as a guy, you risk a maudlin essay on what may be perceived at least by some as one part romantic, what the spiritual masters called "cupidity" (homosexuality). [*GQ* magazine, a lifestyle magazine for urban men, ran an essay on why men don't bond, and one reason, the piece argued, was because guys apparently don't want to appear gay.[2] Even in *The Four Loves,* which includes, arguably, one of the better essays on Christian friendship, C.S. Lewis feels compelled to spend a few paragraphs making a case that its essence is always something other than Eros (romantic love). Lewis describes the physical position of lovers as being face to face, whereas friends are side by side. Lewis wrote, also, that friendship doesn't happen only between two people. Deeper friendships may include three or more. Obviously, Lewis is recalling his Inklings experience (his friendships with Charles Williams, J. R. R. Tolkien, and others).

My religious tradition has discovered in the last quarter century the blessedness of spiritual mentoring, a kind of spiritual friendship. Mentoring tends to be conceived today, though, still as a cousin of the transactional relationship. I ask an older man to mentor me, and he "pours himself into my life." In return, he gets the satisfaction of feeling significant about his life, helping the next generation find itself. My so-called father-wound heals a little.

My tradition has also in recent years conceived of male friendship in terms of "accountability." Men participate in religious accountability groups for prayer and Bible study, and for a "safe place" where they can discuss a wide range of issues from pornography to the Chicago Cubs (both addictions). An acquaintance whose name is in the Rolodex of many executives in his community recently told me that at his fortieth birthday party, sixty-four friends celebrated with him. "I didn't ask the five guys in my accountability group that meets on Friday mornings," he said. "It just got to be too many."

That's as it should be.

Religious accountability groups have never appealed to me. Maybe that's because being asked by an acquaintance, "Did you masturbate over pornography this past week?" didn't feel redemptive. No doubt some find such groups a source of strength. I wouldn't put those relationships in the same raft as friendship, though they can lead to it.

Friends provide accountability as an insight that comes with being fully known over time. While we were shopping for a new car, a friend hit me with the cliché, "Dave, you know the price of everything and the value of nothing." I was in my early thirties, and he had wearied of my thinly disguised envy. I didn't reply. I couldn't. I hated what he had just said. The comment dug its heels into my soul, though he has never brought it up again. Years later I still think about what he said that afternoon. I can't explain fully why I can accept a stinging rebuke from a friend or why it still rolls around in my head today, years later.

BEST FOR THE BELOVED

Aelred of Rievaulx, a twelfth-century Cistercian monk, wrote one of the religious classics on friendship: *Spiritual Friendship*. The book was published as a running conversation between Aelred and several friends, at least one of whom apparently died during the process. I found the dialogue refreshing, mostly because of its premodern, prepsychology, nontransactional hope for friendship. Most popular discussions of friendship accept the patently obvious: women make friends easily; men don't as much. The conversation then immediately morphs into a taxonomy of gender friendship.

While it obviously flourished among monks before Aelred, the Christian spirituality oeuvre before him didn't trumpet same-gender friendships. No doubt part of that was because of the fear of cupidity. I suspect that the deeper issue, though, was that friendship among the monks might corrupt the monastic disciplines. The monks, then, had reason to worry [A twelfth-century monastery had its pettiness and politics, like that of my local school district.]

No doubt a charismatic personality, Aelred acknowledges the dangers of friendship but argues keenly for it as one of God's great gifts in this life. He borrows some of his thinking from Cicero's dominant work on the subject, which was written by the Stoic philosopher around 44 B.C. However, Aelred, a contemporary of the spiritual giant Bernard of Clairvaux, roots all friendship in charity, or what Lewis in *The Four Loves* calls "gift-love."

This is an important point for suburbia folk. Lewis writes, "But Divine Gift-love—Love Himself working in a man [or woman]—is wholly disinterested and desires what is simply best for the beloved."[3] Divine-enabled "gift-love" is like an underground river that flows beneath all relationships, friend or no. Even if you don't make it to my short list of friends, I seek what's best for you. Love like that can only be divine-enabled. Who can do this? Especially if doing what's best for someone doesn't help my business grow?

With divine-enabled love, I don't just add value to you so you can add value to me, the essence of my business model: When you don't add value to me, then I ignore you. In business, the most important thing I can give my top clients is my time. The farther down from what I deem the top, the less time I give you. That may work for building a business and I'm okay with that, but it can empty life of joy.

While few enter the special class of friend, under Christian duty, I treat all with gift-love. I seek the best for all who constitute my community. Aelred says, for example, that a friendship that can cease was never truly a friendship. That seems a little overstated. Elsewhere he says that if you need to break off a friendship, it needs to be "unstitched little by little."[4] The slow unstitching is a good example of the Christian form of gift-love, which flows under all friendship. Even in backing out of a friendship, Aelred believes that it must be done in a way that is virtually imperceptible to the person. That's gift-love. It's the withdrawal of friendship but not the withdrawal of Christ's love.

INSIGHTS OF FRIENDS

How does a friendship begin?

As I look at the handful of those I call friends, I can't answer that. All friendships, likely, began transactionally, in one way or another: one in college, another in graduate school, still another early in my professional career. A couple in recent years. Why them and not others? What constitutes Friendship as opposed to friendship?

As a monk of rank from nine centuries ago, Aelred approaches the topic rationally. I warmed to it slowly. His "stages of friendship" has the emotion of a corporate training manual.

Four are the stages of friendship, he says: selection, probation, admission, and, finally, "perfect harmony in matters human and divine with charity and benevolence."[5] In selection, Aelred thinks the garrulous, those with a bent toward anger, and those who reveal secrets make poor friends. Aelred seems to care about more spiritual character and less about outward piety. In probation, he suggests not forming "intimacies too quickly" because of how painful it is to undo a friendship. The testing stage is crucial, I think, to Friendship in the 'burbs. No doubt there are advantages that come with Friendship (a family weekend at the condo in Vail), but they come after it. Advantages follow Friendship; they never precede it as part of something else.

Nor do they define it. Aelred says to test subtly the intentions of a fresh friendship: What does he really want from me? Status? A referral to a business venture? With the class structure of the suburbs erected from the transactional model of relationships, the testing phase may be the most crucial. Celebrities and the wealthy struggle most with this, I suspect: Does this person really care for me, or only for what I can do for him? Envy, covetousness, and greed never lead to Friendship.

Aelred's stages serve as a check to my emotions. I asked some colleagues to describe Friendship, and one said, "It's just someone with whom you have an 'instant-on.'" An instant-on, though, may not necessarily make it all the way to Friendship, so it must be tested. And what about those who never really experience an instant-on? Instant chemistry may or may not lead to Friendship.

There's nothing particularly religious about Friendship as described by Aelred, other than, perhaps, that the subjects of God and faith unite rather than divide (perfect harmony in matters human and divine). There is a simple, human pleasure in being with someone with whom you do not feel compelled to add value. It is a pleasure of the kingdom of God, anticipating a time when business is over. Aelred writes that a "man never truly loves a friend if he is not satisfied with his friend as he is."[6] In this, the kingdom of God is realized: I don't have to be anything other than who I am.

Many who look to Scripture for glimpses of this quasi-spiritual practice point to David and Jonathon's friendship in the Old Testament and that of the two on the Emmaus

Road in the New Testament. In the Emmaus Road story (Luke 24:13–34), two of Jesus' followers walk from Jerusalem to Emmaus, and the resurrected Jesus joins up with them. I've always liked that the two were walking somewhere. Doing something. Not sitting in church taking the Eucharist or hovering over a Bible at a coffee shop.

The image of the two, unaware that the third is Jesus himself, reminds me of many warm late September days fly-fishing some Montana or Wisconsin stream with a Friend who takes caddis larvae and scud imitations seriously. We move up the river all day long: fishing alone, fishing together. Long are the stretches of silence and conversation. After the evening rise, we peel off our waders. We drive to the nearest local "supper club" for a late dinner. Aelred says that "the best companion of friendship is reverence," and that's how I feel about those days.[7] The holy pours through each moment. There are not two fishing the high mountain lake but three. As C.S. Lewis says in *Friendship,* there is always a little humility on the part of each toward the others; with all my Friends, I feel lucky to be counted as one.

Friendship, says Aelred, tempers adversity and moderates prosperity: "[It] . . . heightens the joys of prosperity and mitigates the sorrows of adversity by dividing and sharing them."[8] I recently received an e-mail from a Friend thanking me for my support during his father's illness. He wrote, "I was searching for something this afternoon when I ran across some e-mails from my dad while he was struggling with cancer. It reminded me again of your friendship. I don't know if I ever adequately said THANKS for all that you did for my dad." I had simply referred his father to a research oncologist, who worked to get him into a clinical trial. I also visited the dying man, a pastor, and his wife a couple of times near the end. My support was, by all measures, unremarkable.

The day of the funeral on the casket hung two baseball caps: the St. Louis Cardinals and the New York Yankees. The pastor loved life, and he had raised four boys who would carry on his sense of balance and wholeness, and his passion for sports. My Friend, the oldest boy, and I chuckled as the pallbearers loaded up the casket and stuffed it into the back of his father's SUV. My Friend drove it the mile or so to the gravesite. As I proceed farther into midlife, my sense is that I'll need my Friends much more for adversity than I will in prosperity.

Perhaps Friendship anticipates God's kingdom, because, finally, it's the relationship with the greatest potential to be blind to race, class, and economics. If all my Friends are just like me, then how many are only of the add-value variety? I live in spiritual poverty if my "starter castle" envy is so great that my Friends possess only the immortality symbols that I feel good about.

NEW COMMUNITY

One of the most penetrating spiritual themes of my life has been feeling like I don't belong. In my head, I'm always the foreigner. I'm on the outside looking in. I've even felt that way about my religious community.

me too!

I don't think it's that I've not felt *wanted* by certain people, such as my parents or siblings or my wife or key father figures. It has always been my position in relationship to a larger community. I never really felt part of one. My family and I have now lived in the same house for more than six years. That's the longest I've lived in one spot, ever. I grew up much like kids whose parents serve in the military. I didn't stay long enough in one community to feel as if I had member status.

When I was fourteen, my parents sent my oldest sister and me to a boarding school on the prairies of South Dakota, about 250 miles from home. Sequestered thirteen miles from the nearest community, the small school was like a monastery. I remember the deathly quiet and empty Saturday mornings on campus, the bitter, below-zero winter wind whipping around and through the cinder-block buildings and a handful of ranch-style houses that squatted low along a desolate and straight Dakota highway.

The lucky students who lived not too far away or had older siblings with cars at the school could go home Fridays and come back Sunday evenings by 9 P.M. My sister didn't have a car. Until I got wheels at sixteen, I spent many Saturdays mostly alone, in my ten by fifteen-foot dorm room, watching TV in the lounge, shooting hoops if someone found a key to the gym. A Friend at the time lived on campus in one of the houses because his parents worked at the school. I envied him. He got to go home after school each day. My most treasured moments of those four years include the few times he invited me home for the weekend, a hundred yards from my dorm room. It may as well have been Hawaii.

Through the years of moving (several times in elementary school, high school, college, graduate school, first job, etc.), I have satisfied at least part of my need to feel like a bona fide member of a community, but not so much through our church (as, for example, my wife does, since she grew up in it). Today I feel wanted by a few Friends, those I feel lucky to have found along the way. I see them as God's provision when I felt as if I had no community status. They are more than just a collection of individual Friends. They are members in my community, where I belong, even though none really knows the others in the circle. I finally have membership.

Not long ago I said to a Friend that I really needed to sense God's presence, that I felt thirsty for something real. I had been through another rough patch with family and business and all the activities that constitute the so-called good life. We had lunch one day, and several weeks later he wrote me an e-mail in which he agreed that yes indeed, life is hard some days: "Yes it is, especially when we begin to experience the loneliness of the human condition and the emptiness within. We naturally reach out to anyone or anything to fill the void. Even God. And when nothing works and God is silent . . . well, then it's time to be quiet and reach out to a friend who needs us."

In Friendship I can say I have *felt* the grace of God, where I have experienced what it means to be accepted not for the value I add but for the value I am.

Good...

In Love with Time

Environmental Toxin: "I need to get more done in less time."
Spiritual Practice: Falling in love with a day

I once visited a thirty-year-old stockbroker on the twenty-fourth floor of a building on La Salle Street, not far from the Chicago Mercantile. He greeted me wearing the financial district's uniform: a dark blue suit with black wingtip shoes. He also sported green marbled cufflinks, which coordinated nicely with his tie. He had an office with a window and the standard cherry furniture.

"You must be 'the Man,'" I said, "to have an office with a window." Outside his open door a herd of stockbrokers on phones milled in and out of gray cubicles.

"I had a good quarter," he said. "But I worked hundred-hour weeks to get here. And being here now is no guarantee I'll keep the office after next quarter."

I did not know the broker well (the relationship began with a cold call from him), but my guess is that each year in the middle of his hundred-hour weeks, he squeezes in some time in Cancun. Play is as managed as his clients' portfolios. Keep the pedal on the floorboard while you're young. Consume life today to enjoy it tomorrow. This is the true religion of the suburbs.

I've never begrudged the pails of money taken home by the indentured class of men and women who work in Chicago's financial district and commute to the outlying suburbs. [Many live in the biggest houses and take great vacations, but their lives are not their own.] If you figure that they may get three weeks of vacation a year (if that) and then do the math on, say, a thirty-year career, that adds up to about ninety weeks of real living. You have to conclude that they are not getting paid enough.

An acquaintance who quit the business in midlife recounted eating alone, his face almost falling into his plate, around eight each evening after a fifty-minute Metra commute back to his big house in the 'burbs, while his lonely wife chased the four kids into bed. He said that when he jumped off the Investment Banker Express, he weighed only 140 pounds. I'd bet he's a good twenty pounds heavier today, more than a decade later, and he's by no means paunchy.

No one sets out to live a chaotic existence; it just sort of happens: one day you wake up and hate your life, but it's another fifteen years before the last kid will be gone or another ten years until retirement or another two years until you're done with your night-school MBA. Or you and your spouse both have successful careers, and neither is about to let go, no matter the stress on the marriage or kids. There seems no way out.

Million are the reasons why the suburbs seem to produce a class of folks who feel trapped. Perhaps it's the unlimited opportunities or the unchecked narcissism or the stubborn refusal to be left behind. Or if you're working a couple of part-time jobs to make ends meet, survival itself creates the chaos; you really are trapped.

As all Christian wisdom figures have said throughout the centuries, however, the busy life is, for the most part, an unreflective life. Many are the reasons why I complain about the craziness of my life and still refuse to do nothing about it. I know my life is out of control. I just need to do something about it. I feel trapped, though. You can't build a business on forty hours a week, right? Besides, it's not only the actual work; it's the space it occupies in your mind; like rain in the desert, thoughts of survival and success seep into every crack and soak deep into the subconscious.

A friend and her husband both work outside the home, and with three active kids—two of them teenagers—their schedules represent the archetype of suburban living. "Tell me what to cut," she says when I ask her how she finds time for rest. She wishes it were different, but there's no way out. She lists all her kids' activities;

nothing, truly, can be cut without "hurting one of the kids." Her professional calling allows little flexibility.

The suburbs are all about saying yes to opportunity and the immortality symbols it promises. Its deep current pulls under your good intentions. You can't simply start swimming to shore by throwing off an activity or two, by saying no. You start with something bigger, like one of the Ten Commandments. In *The Sabbath,* Abraham Heschel writes that instead of coveting things of space (the Tenth Commandment, "Thou shalt not covet"), we must learn to covet time (the Fourth Commandment, keep one day holy). This is the eighth and final soul practice: to pursue an affair with time. To fall in love with a day.

TIME AS CONTROL

I once interviewed the legendary black preacher, Dr. Gardner Taylor, in his home in New York City. Retired as a preacher ever gets, he was in his mid-seventies at the time. His wife of half a century had recently been killed by a city truck as she crossed the street. Dr. Taylor didn't seem bitter. He had that elder statesman sweetness about him. But sadness underlay his comments. "As we grow older," he said, "this life shows its true qualities of impermanence and unreliability. The young ought not feel that way; they ought to have the illusion of permanence. I don't think you could live very well without that illusion. As one gets older, God has ordained it so that as one must leave the world, it becomes less attractive."[1]

It's the very illusion of permanence, though, that often cheats us out of the deeper spiritual life. It's a veil that cloaks a thicker reality. Years fly by with little sense of the precious nature of time and with few experiences of the presence of God.

Time itself is, in many ways, an illusion. The idea that time can be controlled is relatively new, only dating back eight centuries. Before the thirteenth century, inventors had "wasted centuries attempting to measure time by imitating its flowing passage, that is, the flow of water, sand, mercury, ground porcelain."[2]

Time was thought by the masses to be a relentless, arbitrary uncontrollable god. But some monk (yes, it was likely a religious person) with too much time on his hands thought, "Hey, what if I stop thinking of time as a smooth continuum and think of it as a 'succession of quanta.'"[3] So a thirteenth-century European monk revectored the course of Western civilization with what now seems like a simple concept: the escapement, which is made possible by the oscillating device (think: the pendulum motion in grandfather clocks that was developed later). The device broke time up into measurable, regular intervals, like what you hear with the ticking of a watch. Voilà! Time could be counted, measured, and thus controlled. And the next thing you know, moms in large Child Moving Vehicles with Palm Pilots herd their children to ballet at the Park District community center and then run to work out at the local health club for forty-five minutes before dashing back through traffic for a quick stop at Starbucks and then back to the Temple of Potential to pick up the munchkins.

In *Geography of Time,* social psychologist Robert Levine explains that cultures perceive time differently. He divides cultures into those that are event-oriented and those that are schedule-oriented. The inhabitants of countries like Brazil and Ecuador organize their lives around *events.* Thus North Americans who visit there extol the virtues of the "siesta" pace of life. The United States, like many other Western cultures, runs on schedule-oriented time: the schedule controls the pace, not the event. Life is efficient, managed, controlled.

How we experience the tempo of time is local as well as personal. For example, the experience of time (slow or fast) changes from culture to culture, even within Western civilization. Many factors contribute to the tempo of a locale: climate (the hotter the weather, the slower the pace); population size (larger cities experience a faster speed of life than do rural areas); and cultural values (individualistic cultures like the United States move more quickly than, say, community-oriented ones, such as those in South America). The bummer is that economically healthier cultures appear to live life the fastest *and* experience the highest satisfaction with it, but with the exception of Japan, they also apparently have the highest incidences of coronary disease.[4] So go ahead and have some French fries and sign your kid up for *two* Park District sports during the spring season; you truly can't have it all—total happiness *and* no health worries.

Suburbia is where time has been domesticated once and for all. Yet for the most part, it is an illusion, and there's a more satisfying way than consumption to organize your days.

HOLINESS IN TIME

"Sex was so much better *before* I was married."

It was a girlfriends' weekend in the city. My wife and several friends were enjoying a nice dinner *sans* kids and husbands. The evening conversation began with a general discussion about kids and then narrowed into how young kids are today when you have to talk to them about sex. And then one of the women just muttered it under her breath, and the conversation caught fire: "It's like mopping the floor, something you gotta do."

A few days after the weekend, my wife told me about the conversation, and I vacillated between prurient interest (What did the others say?) and trepidation (What did *Jana* say?). The gist of the evening's topic was that sex simply doesn't happen much in married life. Or it happens, but it really isn't convenient. Jana's editorial comment later was that I should feel lucky.

God's gift to married folk seems more like work than it does play. In a schedule-oriented world, "Make love, not war" has become "Make the soccer game on time, not love." The soccer and baseball games and swim meets fill the family calendar, and we never miss one. Making love, at least for married folk, has no immortality symbol attached to it, so why put it on the calendar? Sex is an intruder in a schedule-oriented world.

When my oldest was seven, he and I were headed out the door to a movie when he asked, "Do you play? Do you play when you're an adult?"

I almost gasped at the force of his comment. "Do you think I play?" I asked. Christian didn't say a thing. We walked to the car in silence.

The answer to the efficient, driven, play-deprived suburban life is not necessarily more sex (although I wouldn't argue with that). The answer isn't better boundaries or more aggressive personal goals—practical how-to solutions. At some point, they may provide some help, but the real issue cannot be addressed directly. I shuck one responsibility only to pick up another: the church really needs me this year, and it feels good to be needed. I hear what the preacher says about using my gifts and talents in the church, but the message enervates me. Suburban religion, its programming, and the need for warm bodies to "advance the kingdom of God" seem only to contribute to my problem. It seems like more stuff to feel guilty about.

My religious tradition doesn't say much about my overindulged lifestyle, or if it does, I can't hear what it has to say. It is big on no sex before marriage (the Seventh Commandment), which does a decent job of making the community feel a modicum of guilt. For the life of me, though, I can't remember even a single sermon on the Fourth Commandment, to keep one day holy. Perhaps I'm suppressing or repressing all those sermons (something I've been known to do). There seems to be little residual community consciousness about the Seventh Day, other than a few leftover blue laws—no purchasing alcohol on Sunday, for example, until after noon. We've come a long way since the "no Sunday" contract that my wife's uncle signed in 1945 when he played major league baseball for the Brooklyn Dodgers. He recalls, "I believed that you shouldn't work on Sunday." He refused to pitch on the Lord's Day, and his stance didn't seem to surprise many.

The real answer to the craziness of my schedule-oriented culture is to view time differently. It surprises me, for example, how death reorders a schedule-oriented life. Priorities change, as does the perception of time. I remember the days between my grandfather's death and his funeral, my brother and I killing time ice fishing on the Missouri River in South Dakota. The three or four days seemed like a month. Our large family sat in my grandparents' house (it was January and below zero), eating one brought-over meal of pot roast and scalloped potatoes after another. No one was going anywhere fast.

And why did a close family friend suddenly become an expert on finches after a bout with cancer? What thirty-four-year-old therapist and mother of two reads *Peterson's Field Guide to North American Birds*? Only someone who is waiting for her hair to grow back. Wouldn't you think, though, that someone with cancer would perceive herself to have *less* time and thus be more busy? But the reverse is true. Cancer appears to slow time down, not speed it up.

In *The Sabbath,* Heschel writes, "There is a realm of time where the goal is not to have but to be, not to own but to give, not to control but to share, not to subdue but to be in accord." Heschel writes that "spiritual life begins to decay when we fail to sense the grandeur of what is eternal in time." He calls the Sabbath "holiness in time,"

a "palace in time," and an "eternity in disguise." It's a day not for furthering our opportunities and those of our kids but to liberate ourselves from the pursuit of such things. "Gallantly, ceaselessly, quietly, man must fight for inner liberty," writes Heschel.

Written in the middle of the twentieth century, *The Sabbath* is a trenchant work dominating the spiritual landscape. Only a Jew could have written such a book. My religious tradition loves the other six days, because that's where spiritual entrepreneurship and accomplishment—and thus a sense of purpose—can be pursued. Offhand, I can't think of one true classic on the Sabbath from anyone clearly identified as a Protestant. We produce truckloads of devotionals for our "quiet time" before breakfast (that one sacred time), but we tend to ignore the seventh day, when time as quanta is suspended and eternity sets up shop for a day.

I always thought it strange that in the Old Testament God would force an agrarian community to give up one day a week from working the land. In fact, God threatens the people of Israel with death: "Anyone who desecrates it [the Sabbath] must die" (Exod. 31:12, NLT). That seemed like an economic hardship. Peasant farming is tough enough without a law eliminating one good day of work. But that just goes to show that I'm a modern Protestant in a schedule-oriented culture. I was stunned,

then, at the painfully obvious insight from Judith Shulevitz's *New York Times* article several years ago, which pointed out that the Jewish Sabbath specifically permitted poor people the same luxury for rest as it did for the privileged and wealthy.[5]

The lower class may not have been able to afford a long weekend on the shores of the Mediterranean, but at least one day a week, they didn't have to wipe up the pubic hairs of the rich from the shower stalls. One day a week they entered eternity in time, where all humans were economically equal.

HOLINESS OF PLAY

I grew up in a large family where Sunday morning church was the only option. We arrived home just after noon, and lunch was a large spread that included beef with mashed potatoes and gravy. A two-hour afternoon nap followed. My parents militaristically enforced the Sunday afternoon quiet. We then traipsed back to church in the evening for more hymns and more second-rate preaching. Sunday was a two-a-day—two church services to endure.

Each Sunday, we five kids fought all the way to church, got spanked upon returning home for cutting up

during the church service, and then got whacked again when we woke our parents by bouncing the basketball on the back driveway. Corporal discipline and the Sabbath were synonymous to me.

I can still remember the Sunday in my late teens when I informed my father that I would be water-skiing that afternoon. His face tightened in disapproval, but he didn't enforce the rule of law, that Sunday was not for outdoor recreation. I had finally worn him down. From then on, I abandoned the Sabbath practices of my family, finally liberated, and for the next twenty-five years I treated the Sabbath as just another day out of seven. And not until confronted with suffering of my own making (workaholism) did I begin to add a few of the old practices back into my life.

The first few years of my business, economic survival consumed me. I took my laptop everywhere—including our so-called family vacations. My family suffered through my mercurial phases and an endless string of months with a dad and husband who was a grump. In many ways, the experience tapped into some darkness in me. It wasn't about economic survival only. After having done everything I could, I was simply unwilling to trust the outcome to God. I lived like an atheist. François Fénelon writes, "Is this continual resistance due to the fact that He has not given you what you want in a way that will flatter your ego?" One of Fénelon's themes is that it's not the cross (the hardship we're facing) that causes us so much pain, it's our resistance to the cross. That is, we're fighting the hardship itself—and that adds to our suffering.

A friend rescued my family by giving to me a $160 birthday present: a four-week membership to a "boot camp" at a local health club. The intense early morning exercise, while almost doing me in, resurrected my spirits (with the help of a few meds). Someone once said that change often comes about like this: pain + time + insight = change. My insight was, "This is stupid; no business is worth this."

I also began a discipline, small though it may seem, of not turning on my laptop, cell phone, or anything electronic from Saturday evening to Sunday evening (twenty-four hours). I even stopped watching sports on television for the most part. It could have been any day, but Sunday fit best with our family's station in life. Creating the ritual was excruciating. I arrived home from church many Sundays consumed with sending just one more e-mail. Often I didn't resist. I recall downloading e-mail to my cell phone during one Sunday worship service between the offering and the sermon. I remember the moment, because an e-mail from an anxious client ruined the rest of the worship.

As with all spiritual practices, when I first implemented the twenty-four-hour Sabbath lockdown, nothing much happened. I can't say that my business
prospered as a result of attempting to keep one Sunday
holy. ("I'll force God to bless me by obeying one of the
commandments" is the quid pro quo approach to spirituality.) The schedule-oriented rationale for keeping one
day holy is that I'd be more efficient the other six days.
That's not the essence of the biblical Sabbath.

I began, though, to view my drivenness and anxiety
about my business perhaps as God saw it: as a person in
need of repentance. To give up control. To return owner-
ship of the company to him. And to entrust my future—
and possible failure—to him, no matter the outcome.
Shutting off my cell phone for one day became a simple
act of obedience subverting my illusion that success was
in my hands.

Over time, though, even that measly attempt at a
Sabbath returned to me, a middle-aged suburban male,
the gift of play—much like my sons understand it: a
warm, lazy early fall afternoon of street hockey with the
neighbor boys. The afternoon stretches on and on until
the unwelcomed call to come in for dinner. That notion
of play may come closest to the holiness in time described by Heschel, where time as quanta is suspended,
and I enter a parallel universe. I enter a new universe for

only twenty-four hours, where I am free to play without anxiety about my son's success or my client's project.

Michael Hedges, an exceptional guitarist, died in a car accident in 1997, and his final CD, *Torched,* was released posthumously. The word *torched* is defined on the CD cover "as a noun describing a state of being . . . a state of heightened physical/spiritual awareness."[6] While that may describe the state of someone on peyote, it might also describe someone who has fallen in love with the Seventh Day, fully alive, rested, free from the anxiety of the world.

What Heschel describes in *The Sabbath* is not a day of schedule-oriented church activities, though worship in community is spiritually vital. Nor is he describing what only the rich can do on their long family weekends: fly to Aspen for a couple of days of deep-powder skiing. A true Sabbath is not an amenity of the economically lucky. Perhaps one key measure of whether you're experiencing a true Sabbath is to ask, "Can someone in poverty experience this?"

MENDING

University of Chicago professor Norman Maclean probably never imagined that his book, *A River Runs Through It,* would trigger an avalanche of upper-middle-class suburban white males to his sport. Fly-fishing is almost a cliché now in suburban life; one of the best fly shops in the Midwest is a small storefront a couple of miles from my house, dead-center suburbia.

In the sport of fly-fishing, the primary goal is to cast into the stream or river an imitation of a bug so that it appears to be real—a real mosquito or ant or grasshopper or mayfly. When fly-fishing is done well, a trout spies the imitation rolling along the bottom of the stream, suspended in it, or floating on its surface, and strikes the fly.

The fly-fisher must at all times pay attention to how his or her fly appears under the surface. Since the fly-fisher can't see the fly under the water, he or she watches the floating fly line as it drifts with the current. A common way to cast a fly is to cast it upstream and let it float downstream. The fly-fisher's goal is a "dead drift," where the imitation insect flows naturally with the current.

This is painfully difficult to execute. To create a dead drift, the fly-fisher mends the fly line—continuously makes small adjustments—as the fly floats downstream. Mending is a key activity in effective fly-fishing. The better you are at it, the better the results (the more trout you catch).

Mending is a key image for embracing the Sabbath in the suburbs, letting us "experience the depths of Jesus Christ," as the classic work by Jeanne Guyon puts it. The trick for the lover of God is to learn how to become better at mending one's life, making small adjustments on a regular basis to avoid the speed and clutter of modern living.

Several acquaintances have left suburban life for a three-month or year-long stint as short-term missionaries. When they return, their faces flushed from life abroad, often they downscale their lifestyles, strangely energized. Some return to buy homes with lower mortgages. But I've often noticed that the experience eventually wears off, like a summer tan in early fall. Before long, at least outwardly, they are as before: swept up in the swirl of suburban life. Entropy is nowhere more at work than in one's spiritual energy and good intentions. That's especially true in the suburbs, where the accumulation of activities drives one to exhaustion. Mending reverses this, making small adjustments to our life, constantly paring back that which gloms on to our life in the natural ebb and flow of making life work.

The writer of the Epistles of John often uses the present tense of verbs such as *abide* to suggest ongoing action (also called the continual present). Mending is a verb and a life practice that opens us up to the free and light life offered by Christ. Mending must be an ongoing continual activity. Entrance into the deeper spiritual life is by way of obedience in the small things. And in return we experience a sure fruit of life in the thicker world: inner freedom and peace.

With no social or religious pressure to keep one day holy or even parts of other days holy, mending is personal and situational, like much of religion in Western civilization. With the Park District and sports gods that are now in power, families face hard decisions about the Seventh Day.

A friend with three kids agonized whether to give up Sundays to sports: "If you have a son who is gifted in soccer, do you give up church to allow him to join the traveling soccer league? If you don't, his skills won't fully develop. And also, once he stops soccer, he gives up his community, his friendships." But her church community holds worship services only on Sunday morning. In the end, she and her husband decided to allow their oldest to play with the travel team but not every Sunday, so at least some weeks he can join them in worship. Her son gets benched the next week for the first quarter of the game. It's not much, but it's one small attempt to honor the holiness of time, entrusting God with his future opportunities. She is mending her life, making a small adjustment, to create eternity in time for the family.

Friends in Colorado made a decision not to put their kids in competitive sports during the winter. Winter became holy, empty of competition. Kirk says, "Winter has become our family season. Friends recommended we put our kids in ski school up at Loveland, but after a while we decided that we wanted skiing to be fun, not competitive." For them, winter has become a sort of Sabbath from the pursuit of success, part of their obedience to taste eternity in the midst of time.

Jana and I have tried to mend our lives by keeping sections of the day holy, set apart, a palace in time, such as evenings from six to nine (from the time I arrive home until we herd the kids off to bed). Before that, I got home from work at six, set up my laptop on the dining room table, and downloaded e-mail while the kids were still finishing their meal. My daughter, Kira, kept complaining that she had to ask me a question three or four times before I'd finally acknowledge her by growling, "What do you want?" My children will not think of those years as the best of Mayberry.

We cut out all television on school nights, and we isolated a Family Night, when we made a craft or went out to eat or played a game (even though I hate games). Thanks mostly to Jana, Family Night sticks out in our kids' minds as something special.

The more Jana and I work to mend our lives, the more other "good" activities intrude on our "Sabbaths." I can't determine how active our family should be at church. My wife serves on several committees, which meet evenings and Saturday mornings. Is there a more holy time than evenings and Saturday mornings? We've decided, at present, that I can't serve on the leadership team or another active church committee while Jana is also serving in a similar capacity. Right now, I'm as inactive as I've been at church for years. I confess that it feels pretty good. My Sabbath from church work is only for a season, but it has been a sort of mending as Jana and I seek to build palaces in time.

I once spoke at a Bible study for women on the soul practices of suburban living. After I had pontificated about the values of keeping one day holy, a young mother essentially clucked that as a man I didn't fully grasp how impractical a Sabbath was for a mom of three. As I was choking on my words, a middle-aged woman spoke, "Well, I don't do laundry on Sunday. The kids don't have to do homework on Sunday. We don't go out to eat a lot, but we might do that on Sunday."

Her final words still ring in my ears: "The Sabbath won't come up and embrace you; you have to embrace the Sabbath."

10

Awake

In *The Ends of the Earth,* roving journalist Robert Kaplan describes stopping for tea at a desert oasis in Persia. The oasis, lined with trees, was fed from "a system of underground man-made water channels called *ghanats,* in operation since antiquity."[1] The spiritual disciplines of the Christian faith are like a *ghanat* to your suburb. They are the only means of staying awake to the thicker life amid the toxic fumes of suburban life.

A friend, a software developer, told me, "I jumped around quite a bit before coming to my current job. I was always afraid of something *bad* happening when a situation was not going as I had hoped or expected. So I'd jump ship. I kept up with the folks that hung on in those situations and surprisingly, they all lived! So, when we started in our tailspin here, I thought, *This time I want to ride it out and see what happens.* Change in strategy for me. . . . If anything, spiritually, it was a form of reckless abandonment with the notion that God was in control. Hard in practice though."

With skills as much in demand as his, he needed little from God, at least for his career. But he stayed put at the start-up company, which appeared to be going down or at least going nowhere. What he tasted while waiting was God's provision. He found himself needing God as never before. A simple decision pioneered a frontier that he had rarely explored: giving up a little control to see how God would provide. And it's these frontiers where, it seems, God is most at work—or at least where God can be experienced most.

While the 'burbs can be mocked for being sanitized, sterile, plastic, cookie-cutter, disengaged, rich, racist, white-picket-fence, that's not the nature of the thicker life in the suburbs. The God of Abraham, Isaac, and Jacob is the God of Ranch Road, Painted Pony Circle, and Skyline Drive. God is here; God is active. The real work of the spiritual life in the 'burbs is staying with the practices that keep me awake.

MORTALITY SYMBOLS

Life, then, is found not in immortality symbols but in *mortality* symbols. In *Prayer,* Swiss theologian Hans Urs von Balthasar writes, "Christian contemplation begins at the point where the meaning of the swiftly flowing surface of earthly events is broken to reveal their relation to heaven."[2]

Landing a mortality symbol breaks the swiftly flowing surface of suburban life. A mortality symbol is life after your husband exits the family with your daughter's ballet instructor and you get to pursue your ex-husband for years to pay for child support while you keep downsizing your life and he keeps cursing and threatening you every time you drop off the kids for his weekend with them. A mortality symbol is life after your son almost dies at childbirth and lives, unemancipated, as a special needs child for the rest of his life. A mortality symbol is life after your wife leaves you because of your infidelity. A mortality symbol is losing your professional job at fifty-seven and never really finding another one that is quite as rewarding. A mortality symbol is a year without a job.

With some trepidation, I asked my wife at our fourteenth anniversary celebration what good things she had seen in my life as a result of starting a business, which has become one of my *mortality* symbols. Much had changed since the day more than five years earlier when I told her I planned to quit my secure job, and the following day she told me that she was pregnant with our third child. By our fourteenth wedding anniversary, the business had finally turned upward, and we had passed through several intense years of medical concerns for two of our kids. We weren't out of the woods—you never are in small business—but ahead there appeared to be a clearing.

I feared asking Jana the question because I wondered if any spiritual good had come of those years. She said, in words as encouraging as always, that most of all she thought I had become a more generous person. She listed several instances, and I choked up. I was afraid to hope that she was right. I also asked Jana about the negative, and not surprisingly, she mentioned my anger, which is even today how I react to stress. My anxiety about work surfaces at home in mini-explosions over petty issues. I've prayed to God to take away my anxiety, and it seems that God's answer has been to make it easier for me to ask forgiveness when I go off on someone. This is not really what I wanted: the humiliation that comes from having to apologize regularly to my kids, my wife, and even once to my son's baseball coach.

A father in early midlife recently commented about his special needs son who was approaching his teenage years: "God has been merciful, patient, and steady through our experience with Jacob. I loathe the thought of who I might be had God not brought him into my life." I too loathe the thought of who I might be had I not gone into business, even if I could redesign its trajectory to

Wow,...

provide me with a bona fide immortality symbol. I finally *get* the Old Testament Psalms. All my life I have read the Psalms, where King David and the other psalmists cry out to God. Frankly, before I thought they were emotional wrecks, overwrought artists. Now I understand they had no more options and were experiencing raw human need. The shock to my system was finding out that the presence of Jesus would be found not in met needs but in unmet expectations and perceived need. I experienced, and am experiencing, the end of myself.

For now, I am taking Psalm 77:19 as the basis for my marketing campaign for the spiritual life on Ranch Road: "Your road led through the sea, your pathway through the mighty water—a pathway no one knew was there" (NLT). The context is the people of Israel's saunter through the Red Sea after its parting by God. The preposition *through* (through the sea, through the mighty water) means precisely "through"—and not around, above, outside. *Through* my mortality symbols. *Through* my shallow 'burb existence.

The other insight from Psalm 77 is that the pathway is not obvious—that is, God's provision is a "pathway no one knew was there." You don't know, really, how to get through your mortality symbol. You see the pathway only as it emerges in the rearview mirror. That's the antithesis of the schedule-oriented, life-all-mapped-out culture.

The collateral benefit of finding God in your mortality symbol is that you get to enjoy the immortality symbols that God does provide. The hot pursuit of Ernest Becker's immortality symbols evokes mostly anxiety. Which means you never really get to enjoy them. It's not that those who possess the symbols are patently unhappy because of the symbols themselves, but it's the unreflective pursuit of them, finally, that flattens life.

Psalm 136 features the liturgy "His faithful love endures forever" (NLT) in every other line. One key idea in the psalm is God striking down the mighty kings, taking their land, and then giving it to his people. God snatches up their most prized possession and gives it to those he loves. The psalmist says that God takes from his enemies and gives to his friends.

I'm not saying that those I perceive to have immortality symbols are God's enemies, because I would be numbered among them. I have my share of immortality symbols. I hope Jesus calls me friend. I wonder, though, if those who look for God amid their mortality symbols don't ultimately experience the true joy of possessions, of money, of successful children. Only when you stop the pursuit do you find the joy in the symbols you've been given. To stay awake means staying vigilant for God among your mortality symbols.

ACTIVE SAFETY

The oversized SUV, an immortality symbol in my community, is a metaphor for the true nature of life: I'm not in reality safer just because I ride higher and in a heavier vehicle. It's now common knowledge that in fact in collisions SUVs often have a higher risk of life-threatening head and chest injuries than do much smaller vehicles. People buy SUVs for the *feeling* of safety. It's also a kind of public relations attempt to say, "We're so successful we can handle both the monthly payments and the gas!"

In the *New Yorker,* journalist Malcolm Gladwell wrote a piece on SUV safety and explained the difference between active safety and passive safety. Active safety is illustrated by the high-performing sports car with tight steering and quick acceleration. Passive safety is the lumbering, heavy SUV, slow to react and not engineered for performance. The "active safety" mindset thinks, "I'd rather have a high performing car that responds well so I can miss the semi that just swerved into my lane." Passive safety thinks, "I'm going to get hit by the semi, so I'd rather be in the biggest vehicle possible."[3]

Active safety may be a key metaphor for entering the thicker reality. I might feel safer on Ranch Road (passive thinking) than if I lived, say, in a Middle Eastern city. But I'm not, really. It's a truly radical notion that God can protect (or not protect) your kids anywhere. You may not need, necessarily, a Christian Everything (school, radio station, Family Fun Fair "Halloween" extravaganza, soccer sports camp, bumper sticker) to shield your children so they grow up to love Jesus and buy their own SUV and live in the gated community on the tony side of town.

Jana and I have observed several couples with exceptional children about fifteen years older than ours. Their kids stand out not necessarily because they got into an Ivy League school or landed Fortune 500 jobs. They seem to think differently. They are truly global in mindset. One family has three boys, the oldest of whom is in his mid-twenties. The youngest, nineteen, studies in Ecuador. The middle son now works for a nongovernmental organization (NGO) in Southeast Asia; he was with the Peace Corps until terrorists targeting Americans forced him across the border. And the last time the oldest son phoned home, he was calling from Bahrain.

How do you raise children willing to exchange their Starbucks card for an NGO in Southeast Asia? "We lived in the Middle East," the boys' mother said, "when we were first married. From then on, we knew if we ever got the chance, we wanted to raise our kids abroad. Kids grow up more slowly there. And we wanted to raise world citizens."

When her husband landed an executive position in Jerusalem, they got their chance. She recalls driving their kids to the Arab section of Jerusalem on Friday nights just to get some pizza. (Everything in the Jewish sector shuts down Friday evening for *Shabbat*.) "When you live abroad," she said, "your kids grow up not being afraid of strangers and diversity—and they learn to eat anything."

I asked how she deals with her fears for her children. "I've learned that no news is good news," she said. Her eyes filled with tears as she said that.

Several years ago, she and her husband moved back to the States to our secure suburb. She teaches high school math and coaches a high school tennis team—what any ordinary suburban mom might do after the boys have gone. She admitted that she worried for a time how living in our suburb might negatively affect her youngest, who at the time was in the middle of his high school years. He seems fine now in Ecuador.

There must be something to giving children experiences, not things. Every 'burban parent, after fifteen minutes of watching her child rip open Christmas presents worth six months of wages for many *entire* families throughout the world, has heard, "Is that all?" The only alternative may be a new liturgy of family Saturdays making breakfast and rolling up sleeping bags for the homeless at the church hosting them for the night. Or afternoons moving third-hand furniture into county housing for a refugee family. No doubt, a few parents may see such activities as another scalp for their students' college application. When I served as a youth director and led a youth mission trip, parents said as much: "This will be a great cross-cultural experience that will carry some weight with the admissions committee!" But no matter, the *experience* of participating in life outside the isolation ward of the suburb opens up new spiritual vistas.

The spiritually sedentary and secure life may ultimately be the greatest risk; you never get to experience God at the end of yourself. Taking the responsibility of missing the semi is, I think, the better adventure.

REVERSE FLOW

In Wallace Stegner's moving novel about the lifetime friendship of two couples, *Crossing to Safety*, the narrator, an aging professor, opens the story with himself and his wife visiting their friends in old age. The narrator's wife has polio. The wife of the other couple is dying of cancer. The professor reflects on how life unravels near its end:

Whatever happened to the passion we all had to improve ourselves, live up to our potential, leave a mark on the world? . . . Instead, the world has left marks on us. We got older. Life chastened us so that now we lie waiting to die or walk on canes, or sit on porches where once the young juices flowed strongly, and feel old and inept and confused.[4]

Stegner was himself quite old when he wrote *Crossing to Safety*. The narrator's world-weary musings trouble me, perhaps because I fear, ultimately, a life that doesn't really matter much. A life that leaves no mark on the world. Perhaps that, ultimately, is why immortality symbols hold so much power over me. I fear dying of a heart attack while pushing my top-of-the-line snowblower down my driveway during the first heavy snowfall of the season.

Is that not the classic image of meaninglessness in the suburbs? There I lie at the end of my driveway on Ranch Road, a pain shooting down my arm and across my chest and wishing that my wife would walk out the front door and find me before darkness settles in.

Near the end of his life, the apostle Paul wrote, "As for me, my life has already been poured out as a drink offering to God" (2 Tim. 4:6, NLT). I never really absorbed the implication of that verse until recently: You don't leave your mark on the world, you empty your mark *into* the world. To stay awake means not gathering immortality symbols to yourself but instead emptying yourself into a world of mortality symbols, of suffering. The thicker life is a reverse flow.

Jana and I have been lucky to orbit around a family with a mortality symbol. The husband runs a small business, and his wife works at home with three kids ten and under. They appear to be the model suburban family with most every immortality symbol, if you read only their Christmas letter and look at the happy photo. However, their oldest nearly died as an infant, the doctors giving him no chance to live. First the couple was told the baby would die, and then that if he lived he would be severely handicapped. For years, the child endured a legion of appointments with doctors and numerous trips to the emergency room. Against the odds, the boy lived. Today at ten, with special needs, he attends our elementary school; the last couple of years he has been in our son's class. He and Christian are buddies and play on the same Park District baseball team. He loves to play catcher, and he hates with a passion to lose a game. I think I love that most about him. Baseball is life.

Jana and I respect the couple not because they've done something heroic like launch a foundation for diagnosing the medical condition that their son had. They simply find ways to serve the poor and struggling in their church and community, such as helping at the homeless shelter or setting up a support group for moms of special needs kids. They find time for friends. They are able to laugh even in the pain. They live amid their mortality symbol with grace and honesty and hope.

MONASTERY PRACTICES

I cannot reconcile the safety and predictability of my life with that of most of the rest of the world. I cannot reconcile the intense fall colors in my Midwestern neighborhood—the reds, coppers, golds, yellows, and fading greens—with the urban squalor of a Fourth World city. I praise Jesus for the parking spot in front of Starbucks when he hasn't, apparently, provided the prostitute in nearby Chicago enough money to feed her two kids. Or a better job, for that matter. I try not to think about those kids. Yet even the good life cannot obviate my unease. In *The Message in the Bottle,* novelist Walker Percy's question continues to dog me: "Why does man feel so sad in the twentieth century? . . . Why do people often feel bad in good environments and good in bad environments?"[5]

I'm not sure, but certainly one reason is my stubborn refusal to stop believing that just one more immortality symbol—or a larger one—will make me at least a wee bit happier. What I increasingly know is that you can't conclude much about what you see. So much of what appears to be real in the suburbs—from money to religion—is an illusion. Several years ago, *The Millionaire Next Door* revealed that most millionaires don't look, dress, eat, or act like millionaires.[6] Talk to any financial adviser or mortgage banker (two professionals with insider information on the good suburban life), and they will concur. [those who appear to be rich most likely aren't.] The lesson for the deeper spiritual life is this: from a distance, you can't really tell who is living it and who isn't. Religion sets some clear metrics: worship attendance, giving, service, sexual fidelity, Bible reading and knowledge, whether your kids attend the local Christian school and whether the late model SUV that picks them up plays Christian radio. [But it's hard to tell, really, who is free enough not to pursue immortality symbols and instead is experiencing the deeper, fuller life of Christ.] It just might be the person who has all of the immortality symbols. Wouldn't that be a bummer? He gets the townhouse in Aspen *and* a more meaningful life!

The thicker life is not an immortality symbol. Then again, maybe it is the ultimate immortality symbol, which can be acquired only through the historical spiritual disciplines, no matter the environment. In the late nineties, I read an interview with pop artist Jewell in *Rolling Stone* magazine. She was near the apotheosis of her career, her albums selling millions. She said, "I'm just a person who is honestly trying to live my life and asking, 'How do you be spiritual and live in the world without going to a monastery?'" I don't think you can be spiritual and live in the suburbs without the practices of the monastery. If I had to capture the deeper Christian life in two words, I'd choose *silence* and *service* within the context, of course, of Christian community. In silence, the flow is between God and me. In service, the flow is from me to the world—ergo, back to God. These are not discrete segments of my day, where I sit in silence for a period of time or serve someone for a few hours. Rather, as I experience the depths of Christ's presence, as my conversation with God matures, silence and service become my life; they are not separate activities in my life. That doesn't happen at first, of course. It happens naturally in pursuing over time the rituals of silence and service.

The suburbs require, I think, a kind of fierceness to stay fully awake to God and the work of God in the world. In his small book, *The Soul of Prayer,* published around the time of the First World War, British pastor and theologian P.T. Forsyth employed the term *importunate* to describe how intensely those of faith should pray to God. The word carries the notion of being assertive in demanding a response from God. That is, we can change God's actions in our life by a deeper, more insistent kind of praying—fierce praying. Forsyth believed, as many contemplatives do, that there are times not to acquiesce to the will of God but to struggle against it. He cites Jacob's wrestling with the Angel of the Lord and Job's take-it-on-the-chin approach to God and Satan's duel in the Old Testament. *Importunate* just may be the right adjective for staying spiritually awake. It's a risky prayer that demands that God reveal himself to you even while you haul your kids to swim practice five mornings a week.

When my son Christian began to swim competitively, he impulsively lifted his head to see who was ahead of him in the lane on either side. The reflex, typical of beginners, changed his body angle in the water, slowing him considerably. I begged him—and then berated him—to stop raising his head. Winning is, of course, everything in eight-year-old, B-conference swimming. I finally resorted to bribery: I promised him $5 for every race where I didn't see him do it. Voilà! The next meet he swam four races, I was out $20, and he won two of them.

Although a vibrant Christian spirituality is always experienced in community and friendship, there's a radically personal component to it. You have a lane and a race to swim. Only you can swim your race. To your final breath, you carry out the spiritual practices of the faith and hand out cups of cold water in Jesus' name. And then you let God sort it all out.

In so doing, you are given the Holy Grail, the deeper life in Christ, the fuller, richer, thicker life, as it was truly meant to be lived.

Notes

CHAPTER 1: THE THICKER LIFE

1. Kenneth T. Jackson, *Crabgrass Frontier: The Suburbanization of the United States* (New York: Oxford University Press, 1985), p. 3.

2. Friedrich Nietzsche, "On Redemption," *Thus Spake Zarathustra,* in *The Portable Nietzsche,* trans. Walter Kaufmann (Harmondsworth: Penguin, 1954), p. 250.

3. I believe I first heard the word "thick" in this sense by Will Willimon, formerly dean of the Chapel at Duke University.

4. Thomas F. Hornbein, *Everest: The West Ridge,* cited in *Outside* (October 1998), p. 66.

5. *Outside* (October 1998), p. 64.

6. Ibid.

7. Ibid.

8. Evelyn Underhill, *Mysticism* (New York: Image Books/Doubleday, 1990), p. 123.

9. Annie Dillard, *Pilgrim at Tinker Creek* (New York: Harper & Row, 1974), p. 32.

CHAPTER 2: INSIDE SPACE

1. Mark Kingwell, "Fast Forward: Our High-Speed Chase to Nowhere," *Harper's* (May 1998), pp. 37–48.

2. *Outside* (April 1998), p. 132.

3. The phrase is attributed to the Buddha.

4. Robert A.M. Stern, *Pride of Place* (New York: Houghton Mifflin, 1986), p. 128.

Notes

5. C.S. Lewis, *The Four Loves* (New York: Harcourt Brace, 1960), p. 19.

6. Roland Bainton, *Here I Stand: A Life of Martin Luther* (Nashville, TN: Abingdon, 1990), p. 167.

7. Henri Nouwen, "Moving from Solitude to Community to Ministry," *Leadership Journal* (Spring 1995), p. 81.

8. Abraham Joshua Heschel, *The Sabbath: Its Meaning for Modern Man* (New York: Farrar, Straus and Giroux, 1951), p. 48.

CHAPTER 3: SCUFFLE WITH THE SELF

1. William Kittredge, *Hole in the Sky: A Memoir* (New York: Random House, 1992), pp. 67, 68, 72.

2. Ernest Becker, *Escape from Evil* (New York: Free Press, 1975), pp. 84–85.

3. Anthony Bloom, *Beginning to Pray* (New York: Paulist Press, 1970), p. 46.

4. Frederick Buechner, *Godric* (New York: Atheneum, 1980), p. 142.

5. François Fénelon, *The Seeking Heart*, Library of Spiritual Classics, p. 12.

6. Census data for 2000. Available at www.cityofwheaton.com.

7. Fénelon, *The Seeking Heart*, p. 138.

8. C.S. Lewis, *Mere Christianity* (New York: Macmillan, 1952), p. 94.

9. Fénelon, *The Seeking Heart*, p. 11.

CHAPTER 4: ABOUT-FACE

1. Heschel, *The Sabbath*, p. 90.

2. Jon Krakauer, *Into Thin Air* (New York: Random House, 1997), p. 140.

3. I got this bit of Old Testament knowledge from my long-time buddy and Hebrew whiz, Steve Mathewson (e-mail, March 6, 2004).

4. Bonnie Miller Rubin, "Reading, Writing, Retailing: Field Trips Flock to Stores," *Chicago Tribune,* February 22, 2004, p. 18.

5. Heschel, *The Sabbath*, p. 89.

6. Jeanne Guyon, *Experiencing the Depths of Jesus Christ* (Sargent, GA: Seedsowers, 1975), p. 56.

7. Lesslie Newbigin, *Mission in Christ's Way* (New York: Friendship Press, 1987), p. 2.

8. Economic Policy Institute, 1998, cited in Barbara Ehrenreich, *Nickel and Dimed: On (Not) Getting By in America* (New York: Henry Holt, 2001), p. 3. See also "Hardships in America: The Real Story of Working Families," http://www.epinet.org/books/hardships.pdf.

9. Ehrenreich, *Nickel and Dimed*, p. 101.

10. Bainton, *Here I Stand,* p. 179.

11. Ibid.

CHAPTER 5: REMEMBERING LAUGHTER

1. Robert Kaplan, *The Ends of the Earth* (New York: Random House, 1996), p. 182.

2. Kurt Vonnegut, June 1996 commencement speech at MIT, *The DePaulia,* May 29, 1998.

3. Bloom, *Beginning to Pray,* p. 67.

4. Guyon, *Experiencing the Depths of Jesus Christ,* p. 32.

5. Bloom, *Beginning to Pray,* p. 67.

6. Fénelon, *The Seeking Heart,* p. 26.

7. Quoted in F. Burton Nelson, "Family, Friends and Co-Conspirators," *Christian History* 10, no. 4 (1991).

8. "Nicholas," *Leadership Journal* (Fall 1996), p. 86.

CHAPTER 6: SHIRKER SERVICE

1. David Peterson, "A Conversation with Valerius Geist: Professional Insight into CWD, North American Wildlife Management, and the Future of Hunting," *North Dakota Outdoors* (June 2004), p. 7. The interview was originally published in the Jan./Feb. 2004 issue of the *Rocky Mountain Elk Foundation.*

2. Ibid.

3. Ibid.

4. Available at http://www.us/subsections/reports/fact_sheets/. The figure for the fiscal year ending June 30, 2003, was 54.4 percent. The calculation is based on those who return within three years, so the actual recidivism rate is much higher.

5. Michael Molinos, *Spiritual Guide* (Sargent, GA: Seedsowers, 1982), p. 40.

6. Underhill, *Mysticism,* p. 81.

CHAPTER 7: LASHED DOWN

1. Lewis, *The Four Loves,* p. 21.

2. Dietrich Bonhoeffer, *Life Together: The Classic Exploration of Faith in Community* (New York: Harper & Row, 1954), p. 27.

3. Fénelon, *The Seeking Heart,* p. 23.

Notes

CHAPTER 8: SPIRITUAL FRIENDSHIP

1. James R. Mellow, *Hemingway: A Life Without Consequences* (New York: Houghton Mifflin, 1992), p. 176.

2. Rory Evans, "Love Ya Man," *GQ* (October 2004), pp. 246–49.

3. Lewis, *The Four Loves,* p. 128.

4. Aelred of Rievaulx, *Spiritual Friendship* (Kalamazoo, MI: Cistercian Publications, 1977), p. 101.

5. Ibid., p. 93.

6. Ibid., p. 125.

7. Ibid., p. 120.

8. Ibid., pp. 57, 72.

CHAPTER 9: IN LOVE WITH TIME

1. "Timeless Tension: How Do You Preach the Unchanging Scripture in a Changing World? An Interview with Gardner Taylor and Lee Strobel," *Leadership Journal* 16 (Fall 1995), p. 26.

2. Alfred W. Crosby, *The Measure of Reality* (Cambridge: Cambridge University Press, 1997), p. 80.

3. Crosby, *The Measure of Reality,* p. 80.

4. Robert Levine, *A Geography of Time* (New York: Basic Books, 1997), p. 174.

5. Judith Shulevitz, "Bring Back the Sabbath," *New York Times Magazine*, March 2, 2003, p. 50.

6. Michael Hedges, *Torched* (New York: Windham Hill, 1999).

CHAPTER 10: AWAKE

1. Robert Kaplan, *The Ends of the Earth* (New York: Random House, 1996), p. 231.

2. Hans Urs von Balthasar, *Prayer* (New York: Sheed & Ward, 1957), p. 230.

3. Malcolm Gladwell, "Big and Bad: How the SUV Ran Over Automobile Safety," *New Yorker,* Jan. 12, 2004, p. 31.

4. Wallace Stegner, *Crossing to Safety* (New York: Penguin, 1987), pp. 12–13.

5. Walker Percy, *The Message in the Bottle* (New York: Farrar, Straus and Giroux, 1954), p. 4.

6. Thomas J. Stanley, *The Millionaire Next Door* (Thorndike, ME: G.K. Hall, 1999), p. 7.

Selected Bibliography

Aelred of Rievaulx. *Spiritual Friendship*. Kalamazoo, MI: Cistercian Publications, 1977.

Balthasar, Hans Urs von. *Prayer*. New York: Sheed & Ward, 1957.

Becker, Ernest. *Escape from Evil*. New York: Free Press, 1975.

Bloom, Anthony. *Beginning to Pray*. New York: Paulist Press, 1970.

Bonhoeffer, Dietrich. *Life Together: The Classic Exploration of Faith in Community*. New York: Harper & Row, 1954.

Crosby, Alfred W. *The Measure of Reality*. Cambridge: Cambridge University Press, 1997.

Dillard, Annie. *Pilgrim at Tinker Creek*. New York: Harper & Row, 1974.

———. *Tickets for a Prayer Wheel*. New York: Harper & Row, 1974.

Ehrenreich, Barbara. *Nickel and Dimed: On (Not) Getting By in America*. New York: Henry Holt, 2001.

Fénelon, François. *Let Go*. New Kensington, PA: Whitaker House, 1973.

———. *The Seeking Heart*. Library of Spiritual Classics, volume 4. Sargent, GA: Seedsowers, 1992.

———. *Talking with God*. Brewster, MS: Paraclete Press, 1997.

Forsyth, P.T. *The Soul of Prayer*. Grand Rapids, MI: William B. Eerdmans, 1916.

Guyon, Jeanne. *Experiencing the Depths of Jesus Christ*. Library of Spiritual Classics, volume 2. Sargent, GA: Seedsowers, 1975.

Heschel, Abraham Joshua. *The Sabbath*. New York: Farrar, Straus and Giroux, 1951.

Jackson, Kenneth T. *Crabgrass Frontier: The Suburbanization of the United States*. New York: Oxford University Press, 1985.

Kaplan, Robert. *The Ends of the Earth*. New York: Random House, 1996.

Kittredge, William. *Hole in the Sky: A Memoir*. New York: Random House, 1992.

Levine, Robert. *A Geography of Time*. New York: Basic Books, 1997.

Lewis, C.S. *The Four Loves*. New York: Harcourt Brace, 1960.

———. *Mere Christianity*. New York: Macmillan, 1952.

Mellow, James R. *Hemingway: A Life Without Consequences*. New York: Houghton Mifflin, 1992.

Molinos, Michael. *Spiritual Guide*. Library of Spiritual Classics, volume 5. Sargent, GA: Seedsowers, 1982.

Newbigin, Lesslie. *Mission in Christ's Way*. New York: Friendship Press, 1987.

Percy, Walker. *The Message in the Bottle*. New York: Farrar, Straus and Giroux, 1954.

Peterson, Eugene. *Take and Read*. Grand Rapids, MI: William B. Eerdmans, 1996.

Raban, Jonathan. *Bad Land*. New York: Random House, 1996.

Rohr, Richard. *Men and Women: The Journey of Spiritual Transformation* (audiocassettes). Cincinnati, OH: St. Anthony Messenger Press, 1999.

Stegner, Wallace. *Crossing to Safety*. New York: Penguin, 1987.

———. *Remembering Laughter*. New York: Penguin, 1937.

Storr, Anthony. *Solitude*. New York: Ballantine, 1988.

Underhill, Evelyn. *Mysticism*. New York: Image Books/ Doubleday, 1990.

Additional Resources

JOIN THE THICKER LIFE COMMUNITY

For additional resources, please visit www.deathbysuburb.net, where you'll find lots of free stuff, including

- A discussion guide for your reading group;

- A blog by author David Goetz that is updated regularly;

- A free e-newsletter that includes a column by David Goetz, as well as interviews with others on spiritual practices for the suburbs and stories of those who are not only surviving the suburbs but finding ways to live reflectively; and

- A list of books and websites for further investigation into how to keep the suburbs from killing your soul.

SMALL GROUP RESOURCE

Death by Suburb is a terrific small group resource for studying and discussing the suffocating pressures of living in suburbia.

Eight spiritual practices form the core of the book (starting with Chapter 2). With your small group, you may consider reading one spiritual practice each week and thus creating an eight-week study from the book.

Other resources on www.deathbysuburb.net include a series of downloadable curriculum guides on the classic spiritual disciplines, such as solitude and the Sabbath, as they apply to the suburbs.

Join the growing thicker life community at www. deathbysuburb.net.

Death by Suburb

A Reader's Guide

Starting with Chapter 2 (Inside Space), *Death by Suburb* identifies eight suburban toxins and counters with eight corresponding spiritual practices to overcome the environmental sickness. This reader's guide is primarily for book clubs or reading groups. If you want a small group study, then go to www.deathbysuburb.net and click on "small group resources," where you'll find a free 8-week study on the eight spiritual practices.

For more resources,
including a blog on spirituality, visit
www.deathbysuburb.net.

I

The Thicker Life

KEY QUOTE:

For centuries, the classic spiritual disciplines or practices have enlarged the capacity of ordinary people to engage the Sacred in the ordinary. Spiritual practices are not really a direct route to an awakened God-consciousness. Some days, they seem stupid, quite worthless, just one of the many activities that keep me from God, even. Yet over time, they awaken us to a brave new world that is, ultimately, more satisfying and true to who we are than what we encounter without them.

Discussion Questions

- What's the most maddening part of living in the suburbs?
- Think about living the perfect life. What are you doing? What do you have? How does it all end?
- Do you believe that it's possible to live in suburbia and not capitulate to its values? What would that look like for you?
- Who are some people you think are living the thicker, deeper life?

2

Inside Space

THE TOXIN: "I am in control of my life."
THE PRACTICE: The prayer of silence.

KEY QUOTE:
Making time or space for God is the most basic element of spirituality. You can't stop your busyness, really. You begin to open your life to God in small amounts.

Discussion Questions

- How do you try to control your life? Or, if that is too personal, how do you see others trying to control their lives?
- Why is solitude and silence so difficult to implement in your life?
- Do you have friends or acquaintances who model the discipline of solitude amid a busy suburban life? How would you describe them?
- What are some of life's deeper questions that may surface during times of silence?

3

Scuffle with the Self

THE TOXIN: "I am what I do and what I own."
THE PRACTICE: The journey through the self.

KEY QUOTE:
The war within—the battle with the self—is really prayer
itself. It's the long struggle to see Goodness and Beauty in
a bogus world.

Discussion Questions

• What are some of the key immortality symbols in
your suburb?

• How does the ugliness of the self surface in the suburbs? One example, of course, is the hyper-competi-
tion among parents regarding their brilliant students.
It's not really about the students, it's about the parents. What are some other faces of the self in 'burbia?

• The most basic element of Christian spirituality is
that, because of faith, God is within you, and thus
the pursuit of God is an interior journey. How does
that strike you? How does that compare with your
understanding of the Christian faith?

4

About-Face

THE TOXIN: "I want my neighbor's life."
THE PRACTICE: Friendship with those who have no immortality symbols.

KEY QUOTE:
The suburbs seem to promote a kind of vigilance on the possessions of others. It includes both a hyperconsciousness of self and a hypervigilance on the possessions of others. It's ubiquitous, heightened vigilance. I'm eternally on point to compare myself to those I perceive have more than I. I'm always weighing my immortality symbols against others'.

Discussion Questions

- What are some practices that you've found helpful in countering the invisible pressure to possess that which you don't yet have?
- Do you have any friendships with people who would be considered poor or disabled? What have you learned from them?

- The meaning behind the word *repentance* is to take a spiritual U-turn. You turn and face the opposite direction. What makes turning our attention from those who have more than we do to those with less (money, power, and privilege) so excruciatingly difficult?

5

Remembering Laughter

THE TOXIN: "My life should be easier than it is."
THE PRACTICE: Accepting my cross with grace and patience.

KEY QUOTE:
I want the thicker life in Christ, but I don't want to address the hard reality of my life. Even in suburbia, life is hard.

Discussion Questions

- Do you agree with the assumption that "life is hard"? Why?
- Do you agree with the point that to fully enjoy life you must fully embrace and come to terms with the suffering that has come into your life? What might that actually look like?
- What kinds of suffering have you experienced? What have you learned about yourself? About God?

6

Shirker Service

THE TOXIN: "I need to make a difference with my life."
THE PRACTICE: Pursuing action, not results.

KEY QUOTE:
I confess that I am a Shirker. I want results when I serve the poor, the imprisoned, the destitute. I want results because I want to make a difference with my life. What good is serving the poor if they don't help themselves and turn their lives around?

Discussion Questions

- What is often behind the drive to make a difference in this life? What's so bad about wanting to make a difference with your life?
- As you evaluate your service in church or in the community, how are you developing relationships with the poor? What have they taught you about God?
- What one activity or act of service could help you begin a relationship with someone who is bereft of any immortality symbols and who needs, mostly, your prayers?

7

Lashed Down

THE TOXIN: "My church is the problem."
THE PRACTICE: Staying put in your church.

KEY QUOTE:

Without a long-term attachment to a local church, there
is little spiritual deepening. The maddening frustration
that prompts someone to leave one church for another
may be precisely the experience that triggers spiritual
progress, if one stays.

Discussion Questions

- What role does church play in your life?
- Have you found the church to be a source of deep relationships? Or place of hurt? Why?
- Think about the different churches you have attended through the years. Is your relationship with
God that much closer as a result of attending one of
them? How do you measure that?

8

Spiritual Friendship

THE TOXIN: "What will this relationship do for me?"
THE PRACTICE: Building deep and meaningful friendships.

KEY QUOTE:
Friendship subverts the system of power, how things get done in the 'burbs and the class system organized around symbols of immortality.

Discussion Questions

- How do you see the transactional nature of relationships at work in your suburb?
- How many people would you describe as a Friend, based on this chapter?
- How have you seen God at work in your Friendships?

9

In Love with Time

THE TOXIN: "I need to get more done in less time."
THE PRACTICE: Falling in love with a day.

KEY QUOTE:
The suburbs are all about saying yes to opportunity and the immortality symbols it promises. Its deep current pulls under your good intentions. We must learn to pursue an affair with time itself, to fall in love with a day.

Discussion Questions

- Was there a time in your life where you felt the pace of life was just right? Describe the time.
- What is behind the feeling of being trapped—"I can't cut anything without hurting one of the kids"?
- What would you have to do to create a real Sabbath in your life?

10

Staying Awake

KEY QUOTE:

The suburbs require a kind of fierceness to stay fully awake to God and to the work of God in the world...To your final breath, you carry out the spiritual practices of the faith and hand out cups of cold water in Jesus's name. And then you let God sort it all out.

Discussion Questions

- What are some of the reoccurring, overarching themes of *Death by Suburb?*
- How might your life be different if you implemented some of the practices, such as finding time for silence or creating a Sabbath in your life?
- What is the one practice that you feel most hopeful about implementing in your life?

For more resources,
including a blog on spirituality, visit
www.deathbysuburb.net.